geometrics
a new way to crochet

an introduction to dragon curves,
golden ratio, and Fibonacci sequence

by ruthie marks

credits

Produced by:

Kooler Design Studio
399 Taylor Blvd., Suite 104
Pleasant Hill, CA 94523
kds@koolerdesign.com

Production Team
- Creative Director, Donna Kooler
- Editor-In-Chief, Judy Swager
- Technical Editor, Marsha Hinkson
- Technical Editor/Proofreader, Shelley Carda
- Book Designer/Illustrator, María Parrish
- Photographer, Dianne Woods
- Photo Stylist, Basha Kooler

Published by:

LEISURE ARTS
the art of everyday living

Copyright ©2006 by Leisure Arts, Inc.,
5701 Ranch Drive, Little Rock, AR 72223
www.leisurearts.com

Made in the United States of America. First Printing.
International Standard Book Number: 1-60140-144-2

about ruthie

Ruthie Marks is a Southern California native and southpaw who learned to crochet about 10 years ago after an early retirement. She lives in Ojai, California with her husband Roger and their three cats, all of whom consider themselves expert yarn wranglers. "I didn't learn to crochet earlier because I couldn't find a teacher who was left-handed. But when I came to Ojai, I discovered a right-handed group of ladies who just sat me down and taught me anyway," she says. Ruthie has been designing professionally for the last seven years. To date she has published nine books, including *Crochet in Bloom, Ruthie's Crocheted Accessories, Ruthie's Easy Crocheted Scarves, and Ruthie's Easy Crocheted Afghans.* Many of her other designs have also appeared in various hard- and soft-cover books and crochet magazines.

contents

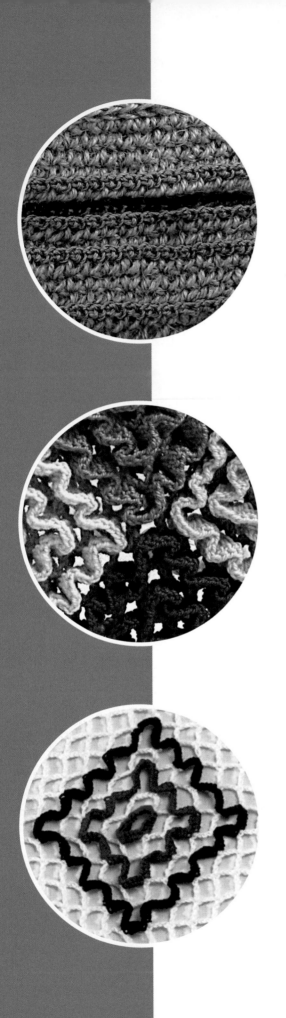

chapter 3 fibonacci sequence

for your information

musings & thanks

The first thing you need to know is that I'm a math-phobe. Geometry scares me half to death and makes my mind freeze. At the same time it fascinates me, especially when I see ways to incorporate it into crochet, and this has helped me to tame the wild beast.

It all began in a Texas antique shop. It was there that I first spied an example of what I later saw referred to as ruffles and wavelets, in the form of a crocheted hot pad. After that I began to gather other samples, patterns, and pictures and put them in a folder marked "Texas Trivet." Eventually I discovered www.woollythoughts.com and found out my fascination had a name – dragon curves! I couldn't have been more delighted and excited. I checked out other websites and entered a whole new world.

Then my good friend and mentor, Gloria Tracy, got me hooked on the golden ratio and the Fibonacci sequence, and suddenly I had three math concepts nagging at me to explore them through crochet.

So here's my first "geometry" book, an introduction to these three concepts. Each chapter starts with a simple project and then builds on it, getting a little more challenging as you go along. Then, when you're ready, there's a list of more advanced projects at the end of each chapter that will take you far beyond the basics and into wonderfully creative spaces.

The second thing you need to know is that I'm left-handed. Everything in this book has been crocheted by me and will look "backward" to right-handed crocheters. But don't worry, all the charts and photographs and drawings, when necessary, are provided for both left-handed and right-handed crocheters.

There are several people I'd like to acknowledge. Susan Levin, another mentor and good friend, who reminds me to not take my crochet self so seriously: "This isn't rocket science," she points out. Donna Kooler and her staff at Kooler Design Studios, who are not afraid to take risks with new designers; Peggy Wells at Brown Sheep Yarn Company, JoAnne Turcotte from Plymouth Yarn Company, Kathleen Sams at Coats & Clark, Doris Erb from Patons, and the Lehigh Group, who provided yarn for the projects. Lucille Merkel and all the right-handed ladies at the local senior center who taught me how to crochet; and my husband Roger Conrad, who believes in me and supports me always.

Introduction

The projects in *Geometrics* were created using three well-established formulas. Don't panic, the book isn't about hard-to-understand mathematical equations, and there will be no tests. We're going to take these concepts apart and play with them so we understand them, then use them to create fabulous crocheted projects of all kinds.

The concepts — golden ratio, Fibonacci sequence, and dragon curves — have been around for a *looong* time. Here are brief explanations:

550 BC: In Greece, Theano, wife of Pythagoras, came up with the idea of the "goldens" — golden ratio, golden cut, golden rectangle, and a host of others. Simply stated, it means that the most visually attractive space is divided into proportions of approximately ⅔–⅓. Notice I said this was Theano's theory. In ancient Greece, women weren't given credit for much of anything, so the recognition went to her husband.

1202 AD, Italy: Leonardo of Pisa, also known as Fibonacci, has been called the "greatest European mathematician of the Middle Ages." In 1202 he published his book *Liber Abaci*, introducing the western world to the decimal system of mathematics that replaced Roman numerals, and to the numerical sequence that bears his name: 0–1–1–2–3–5–8–13–21 etc. The sequence keeps building on itself by adding together the two previous numbers.

1890: Giuseppe Peano, another Italian, first explored the idea of space-filling curves. Others came along later to refine his theory, and that's how dragon curves came to be. Though computers are used to construct truly advanced dragons, you can easily test the basic concept. Fold a thin strip of paper crosswise, again and again. Then release it and watch how it expands. The more folds there are, the more the paper fills up the space and begins to look like a dragon!

Golden ratios, Fibonacci sequences, and dragon curves have very precise rules, but this book is not about absolutes. It's a less structured introduction to these basic principles, using fun and easy-to-create projects. You will learn how to bend the rules whenever necessary to accommodate a design.

The golden ratio and the Fibonacci sequence are so closely aligned you'd think they were developed by the same person. Obviously, they weren't. But both systems end up using the same percentages, and percentages can be cumbersome. To simplify things, all numbers in the book have been rounded up or down to the closest whole number. For example, 25.92 = 26, and 16.42 = 16. Ready? Let's turn the page and get started.

chapter 1

dragon

curves

dragon curves

Dragon curves are utterly fascinating creatures with endless possibilities. Here's how to make them.

Use a page of a newspaper for an extra long piece of paper. Cut a 1"–wide strip. Always folding in the same direction, fold the strip in half crosswise, once, and crease it sharply. This is a level 1 dragon (1 fold, 2 segments).

Fold in half again for a level 2 dragon (2 folds, 4 segments). Fold in half again for a level 3 dragon (3 folds, 8 segments). Fold in half again for a level 4 dragon (4 folds, 16 segments). Fold in half again for a level 5 dragon (5 folds, 32 segments).

If you unfold your strip after each step, and look down on the edges, here's what they'll look like

(see levels 1-5 on opposite page). Notice that some sides touch, but they never cross over one another.

The more you fold, the more complex the dragon becomes. By level 10, the beast really begins to emerge! (See opposite page).

Obviously, making dragon curves can get very complicated. But remember, this book is an introduction to new forms of artistic expression, not a math lesson, so we're not going to take ourselves that seriously. We're going to simplify and have some fun as we crochet our way through the chapter. Then, check out the Challenges section on page 34.

If you want to get into the thick of things, check out the Resources section on page 111 for books and

websites that will take you as far as your mind will allow you to go. It's a fabulous journey!

Throughout the chapter, when needed for clarification, instructions for left-handed crocheters (LHC) and right-handed crocheters (RHC) are included. Usually the instructions are the same for both. When there is a difference, everyone begins on the same leg, but LHC start on the left at the red dot and work clockwise. RHC start on the right at the green dot and work counterclockwise.

In the following pages dragon curves are used in a variety of ways: to cover the entire surface (doormat), on every other row (tote), and on selected areas only (scarf, shawl, afghan, and labyrinth).

dragon curve levels

level 1   level 2   level 3   level 4   level 5

level 10

luxury scarf

Your introduction to dragon curves is to make a continuous zigzag back and forth across short rows on each end of a scarf, using an open mesh as a canvas on which to create.

skill level

Easy

size

3" x 48"

materials

Sport Weight Yarn (1.75 ounces/184 yards, 50 grams/165 meters per skein):

Teal – 1 skein
• Crochet hook, size E/4 (3.5 mm) or size needed to obtain gauge
• Tapestry needle to work in ends

gauge

7 rows = 3", (dc, ch 2, dc, ch 2, dc) = 1"

instructions

Foundation Row: Ch 271.

Row 1: Dc in seventh ch from hook (counts as first dc and ch-2), *ch 2, sk 2 ch, dc in next ch, rep from * across. Turn — 268 sts (90 dc and 89 ch-2 sps).

Rows 2–7: Ch 5 (counts as first dc and ch-2), dc in next dc, *ch

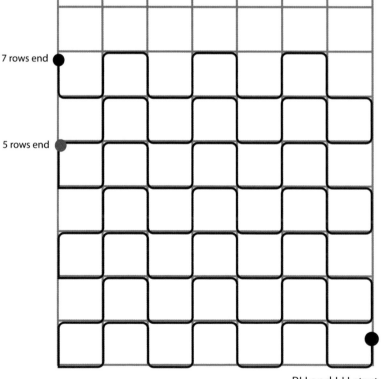

7 rows end

5 rows end

RH and LH start

2, sk 2 ch, dc in next dc, rep from
* ending with ch 2, sk 2 ch, dc in
top of tch. Turn.
Fasten off at end of the last row.

dragon curves
SIDE 1 (LH and RH)
Following chart, zigzag across
and back again as follows: Attach
with sl st, ch 3 (counts as first dc),
3 more dc down same edge. Turn
work, 4 dc across next edge. Turn
work, 4 dc up next edge. Turn
work, 4 dc across next edge. Turn
work, 4 dc down next edge. Turn
work, 4 dc up next edge. Turn
work, cont in this manner across
to end. Work for a total of five
rows. Fasten off.

SIDE 2
Work as Side 1 for a total of seven
rows. Fasten off.

diamond shawl

Wrap yourself up in a soft, sensuous shawl beaming with a sprinkling of colorful dragon curve flowers. Good for any season of the year — lightweight and perfect for a cool evening.

skill level

Easy

size

56" across top, 28" from center of top to bottom of triangle

materials

Sport Weight Yarn (1.75 ounces/184 yards, 50 grams/165 meters per skein):

Natural (A) – 3 skeins
Green (B) – 1 skein
Light purple (C) – 1 skein
Dark purple (D) – 1 skein
• Crochet hook, size F/5 (3.75 mm) or size needed to obtain gauge
• Tapestry needle to work in ends

gauge

3 rows = 2", (tr, ch 3, tr, ch 3, tr, ch 3, tr) = 2"

instructions

Row 1: Ch 8, dtr in first ch. Turn — 1 square (bottom point made).
Row 2: Ch 8, tr in dtr (triangle edge mesh made), ch 3, tr in fourth ch of row 1, ch 3, dtr in same ch (triangle edge mesh made). Turn — 3 squares.
Row 3: Ch 8, tr in dtr (triangle edge mesh made), *ch 3, sk 3 ch, tr in tr, rep from * one time, ch 3, tr in fourth ch of ch-8 at beg of row 2, ch 3, dtr in same ch (triangle edge mesh made). Turn — 5 squares.
Row 4: Ch 8, tr in dtr, *ch 3, sk 3 ch, tr in tr, rep from * three times, ch 3, tr in fourth ch of ch-8 at beg of row 3, ch 3, dtr in same ch. Turn — 7 squares.
Row 5: Ch 8, tr in dtr, *ch 3, sk 3 ch, tr in tr, rep from * five times, ch 3, tr in fourth ch of ch-8 at beg of row 4, ch 3, dtr in same ch. Turn — 9 squares.
Rows 6–38: Continue in pattern as established — 75 squares. Do not fasten off. (After dragon curves have been added, continue with edging from this corner.)

dragon curves

1. Following chart for placement, work all green center squares first

to ensure correct placement of flowers.

2. Hold work as if you are inside looking out, so the back of the sc ends up on the outside of the flowers.

3. Join with sc on first leg, 3 more sc on same leg. Turn work, 4 sc on next leg. Turn work, cont in this manner to end of dragon curve, sl st last sc to first sc. Fasten off.

edging

Ch 3 (counts as first dc), going around edge stitches, 7 dc in corner sp, 5 dc in each ch-4 space down one side, 9 dc in bottom corner, 5 dc in each ch-4 space up next side, 14 dc in next corner, dc into each tr and each ch across to first corner, 6 more dc in first corner sp, sl st to beg ch-3. Fasten off.

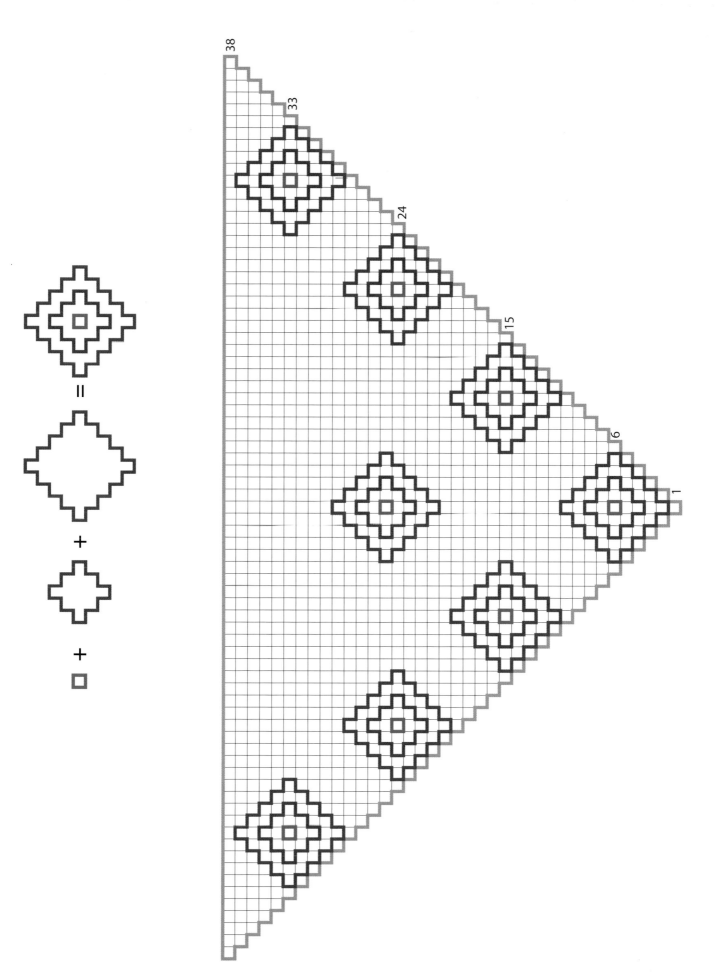

craft tote for all reasons

(including PIGS, UFOs and WIMs*)

Every crocheter needs a bag to carry that PIP (Project in Progress) in the car, on a plane, at the beach. Here's the perfect solution: a generously sized tote that can hold a lot of stuff. The design fills every other row with a dragon curve.

skill level

■ ■ □ □

Easy

size

16" x 17"

materials

Worsted Weight Yarn (3.5 ounces/200 yards, 100 grams/183 meters per skein):

Orange (A) – 2 skeins
Lemon (B) – 1 skein
Magenta (C) – 1 skein
Lime (D) – 1 skein
• Crochet hook, size H/8 (5 mm) or size needed to obtain gauge
• Two 12" pieces of rigid hollow tubing: ½" outer diameter, ¼" inner diameter
• Two ¼" x 2' lengths of yellow cording
• Four 12" lengths of thread to match cording
• White glue
• Scissors
• String or wire
• Tapestry needle to work in ends

gauge

3 rows = 2", (dc, ch 2, dc, ch 2, dc, ch 2, dc) = 3"

chart notes

(See chart on page 20)
1. LH starts at red dot and works from L to R.
2. RH starts at green dot and works from R to L.

instructions

FRONT AND BACK (MAKE 1 OF EACH)

Foundation Row: With A, ch 68.

Row 1: Dc in eighth ch from hook (counts as first dc and ch-2), *ch 2, skip 2 ch, dc in next ch, rep from * across. Turn — 64 sts (22 dc and 21 ch-2 sps).

Row 2: Ch 5 (counts as first dc and ch-2), dc in next dc, *ch 2, skip 2 ch, dc in next dc, rep from * ending with ch 2, skip 2 ch, dc in top of tch. Turn.

Rows 3-24: Rep row 2. Fasten off after the last row.

dragon curves

Following chart for placement and color, attach yarn with a sl st, ch 3 (counts as first dc), 3 more dc on first leg, rotate fabric, *4 dc on next leg, rotate fabric, rep from * throughout. Fasten off at end of each curve.

edging for front and back

Note: Match yarn to side working on.

Row 1 (WS): Attach yarn with sc, 2 more sc around first bar, *ch 3, skip 4 dc, 3 sc around next bar, rep from * to end. Fasten off. Rep for rem 7 sides of both pieces.

Row 2 (RS): With WS facing each other, and working through Front and Back at the same time, attach with sl st in first sc, sl st into next

2 sc, *sl st into next 3 ch by going under 2 strands, sl st in next 3 sc, rep from * to end. Fasten off.

handles

1. Weave plastic tubing through top rows of Front and Back – behind curves, in front of skipped dcs. There will be 10 dc on the back side of the tubing. On the inner side of one handle, attach matching yarn around stem of first dc with sl st, (ch 3, sl st around next dc) four times, ch 6, sl st around next dc, (ch 3, sl st around next dc) 4 times. Fasten off. Rep for other handle.

2. Ends of each cord: Knot thread around cord ½" from end. Add glue to area. Wrap 2 thread strands held tog as 1 around the cord and over the knot. With fingers distribute glue evenly to the area, applying more if necessary. Let dry 20 minutes.

3. With scissors trim end mesh of cord that extends beyond thread. Dip end in glue and work glue into end mesh. Let dry 20 minutes. Rep for all ends.

4. Tape one end of cord to a piece of string or wire and pull cord through hollow tube. Rep for other handle. Adjust cords so all 4 ends are even. Decide how long you want the handles to be and tie a square knot at that spot, using all 4 cords (see photos on next page). Tie from 1 to 4 figure eight knots (see photos) on each side of the square knot, working each end separately or with 2 adjacent ends tied tog (model has 2 adjacent ends tied tog).

*PIGS = Projects In Grocery Sacks. Add to that UFOs (Un-Finished Objects) and WIMs (Works In Mind), and you have a tote for all reasons.

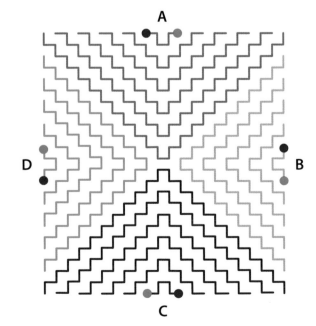

how to make a square knot

1. Place rope B over rope A.
2. Cross rope A over and around rope B.
3. Bend ropes A and B back towards standing ends and bring rope B over rope A and through loop.
4. Holding both ends of rope A in left hand and both ends of rope B in right hand, pull ropes sideways to tighten.

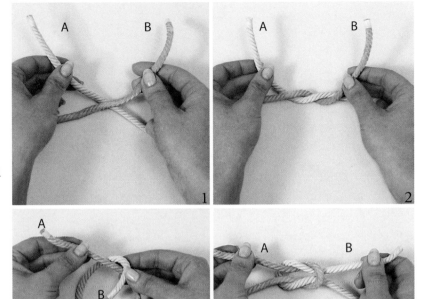

how to make a figure-8 knot

1. Bend the cord creating a loop.
2. Holding ends tightly in left hand, take the loop with right hand and make two half twists.
3. Pass one end back through loop.
4. Pull both ends to tighten the knot. **Note:** If you don't get the figure-eight shape the twists are not correct.

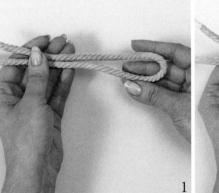
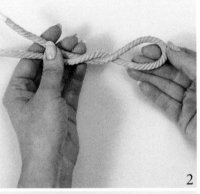

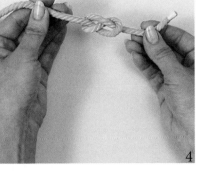

jute
doormat

Jute is the perfect material for a doormat
and demonstrates a practical application
of an elegant design. Put it outside and
watch your visitors appreciate a piece of
art when they cross your threshold.

skill level

Easy

size

15.5" x 25" (a golden rectangle!)

materials

2 FINE Worsted Weight Jute Twine (3.6 oz./75 yards per ball): Natural – 7 balls
• Crochet hook, size J/10 (6 mm) or size needed to obtain gauge
• Tapestry needle to work in ends

gauge

1 row = 1", (dc, ch 2, dc) = 1"

notes

Because jute is a coarse fiber, if you find it harsh on your skin you may wish to wear a pair of light cotton or Spandex gloves. If jute is too difficult for you, use cotton yarn and create a bath mat in-stead. In that case, you may want to increase the size, just be sure to end up with an uneven number of ch-2 spaces and an uneven number of rows.

instructions
base

Foundation Row: Ch 73.

Row 1: Dc in seventh ch from hook (counts as first dc and ch-2), *ch 2, sk 2 ch, dc in next ch, rep from * across. Turn — 70 sts (24 dc and 23 ch-2 sps).

Row 2: Ch 5 (counts as first dc and ch-2), sk 2 ch, dc in next dc, *ch 2, sk 2 ch, dc in next dc, rep from * ending with ch 2, sk 2 ch, dc in top of tch. Turn.

Rows 3–17: Rep row 2. Fasten off at the end of last row.

dragon curves
Notes:

1. Follow chart. Center dragon curves 1-8 are worked in rounds; side curves 1-11 are worked in zigzag rows.

2. On all dragon curves, leave a 6" tail at beg and end for working in ends.

Center

Rnds 1–8: Attach with a sl st on first leg, ch 3 (counts as first dc), 2 dc on same leg, *turn work, 3 dc on next leg, rep from * around, sl st to top of beg ch-3. Fasten off.

Side 1

Rows 1-3 (work from one long side to the other): Attach with a sl st on first leg, ch 3 (counts as first dc), 2 dc on same leg, *turn work, 3 dc on next leg, rep from * across. Fasten off.

Rows 4-10 (top corner group): Same as rows 1-3, except LHC goes from 1 long side to 1 short side and RHC goes from 1 short side to 1 long side.

Row 11 (corner): Attach with a sl st, ch 3, 5 more dc in corner. Fasten off.

Rows 4-11 (bottom corner group): Rep top corner group, except LHC goes from 1 short side to 1 long side and RHC goes from 1 long side to 1 short side.

Side 2

Rep side 1.

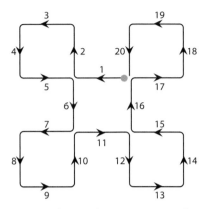

Round 1, RHC start at green dot

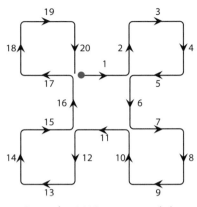

Round 1, LHC start at red dot

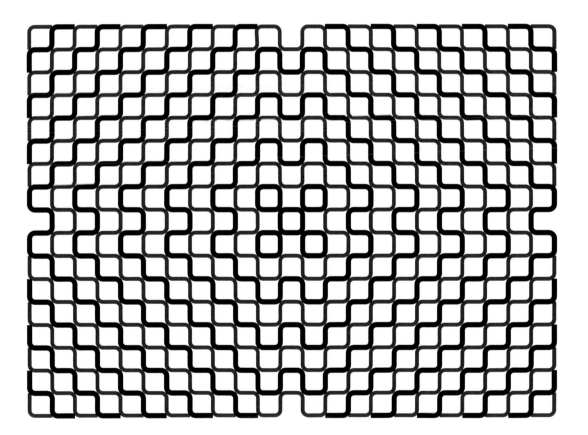

ruffles afghan

A combination of close and open stitches helps the afghan hold its shape, but an overall mesh stitch would also allow for more surface embellishment. Either would work — try them both!

skill level

Intermediate

size

40" x 65" (3 golden rectangles!)

materials

Sport Weight Yarn (1.75 ounces/184 yards, 50 grams/168 meters per skein:

Blue (A) – 10 skeins
Orange (B) – 8 skeins
• Crochet hooks, size G7 (4.5 mm) and G/6 (4.25mm)
• Tapestry needle to work in ends

gauge

9 sts and 4 rows = 2"

notes

1. To change color see notes on page 104.

special stitch

Crossed dc (Xdc): Sk one st, dc in next st, dc in skipped st.

instructions

Foundation Row: With larger hook and A, ch 177.

Row 1: Dc in third ch from hook (counts as first dc), *(Xdc over next 2 ch, dc in next ch) 12 times, [ch 2, sk 2 ch, dc in next ch — mesh insert made] 11 times; rep from * once, rep between ( ) once. Turn — 175 sts.

Row 2: Ch 3 (counts as first dc), *(Xdc over next 2 dc, dc in next dc) 12 times, [ch 2, sk 2 dc, dc in next dc — mesh insert made] 11 times; rep from * once, rep between ( ) once. Turn.

Rows 3–82: Rep row 2, drop A, pick up B.

Rows 83–132: With B, rep row 2. Fasten off.

dragon curves

With smaller hook, follow chart 1 for blue side of afghan, chart 2 for orange side of afghan.

edging (worked with the top side of the afghan facing)

1. Rnd 1, work A on A and B on B. Rnds 2–3, work B on A and A on B.

2. Start on left side at color change (top of afghan is to your right).

3. LH work clockwise, RH work counterclockwise.

LH Rnd 1: With smaller hook attach B with sc around first edge st, sc around same st, 2 sc around each ch-3 or dc stem to corner, 3 sc in corner st, 1 sc in each dc and 2 sc in each ch-2 sp to next corner, 3 sc in corner st, 2 sc around each edge st to color change, drop B, pick up A, 2 sc around each edge st to corner, 3 sc in corner st, sc in each foundation ch, 3 sc in

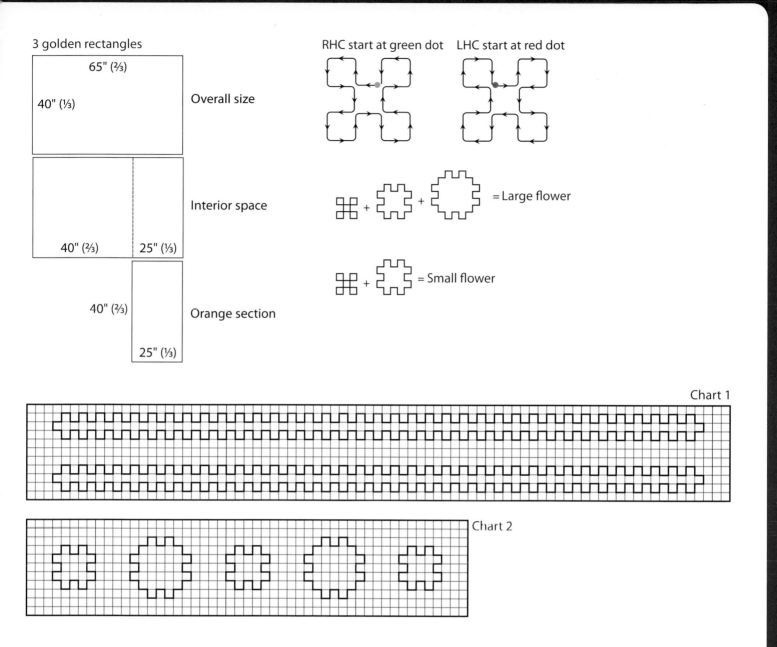

3 golden rectangles

65" (⅔)

40" (⅓)

Overall size

RHC start at green dot   LHC start at red dot

Interior space

40" (⅔)   25" (⅓)

= Large flower

40" (⅔)

Orange section

25" (⅓)

= Small flower

Chart 1

Chart 2

corner st, 2 sc around each edge st to color change, sl st to beg sc. Fasten off.

RH Rnd 1: With smaller hook attach A with sc around first edge st, sc around same st, 2 sc around each ch-3 or dc stem to corner, 3 sc in corner st, sc in each foundation ch, 3 sc in corner st, 2 sc around each edge st to color change, drop A, pick up B, 2 sc around each edge st to corner, 3 sc in corner st, 1 sc in each dc and 2

sc in each ch-2 sp to next corner, 3 sc in corner st, 2 sc around each edge st to color change, sl st to beg sc. Fasten off.

LH and RH
Rnd 2: Attach yarn with a sl st in second sc, ch 3 (counts as first dc), dc in skipped sc (Xdc made), *Xdc across to next corner group, [sk 1 sc, (dc, ch 1, dc, ch 1, dc) in corner sc, sk 1 sc = corner], Xdc across to next corner group, make corner, Xdc to color change,

change colors, Xdc to next corner group, make corner, Xdc to next corner group, make corner, Xdc to beg of round, sl st to beg ch-3.
Rnd 3: Ch 1 (counts as first sl st), *sl st in each st to corner, [sl st in dc, 2 sl st in ch-1 sp, sl st in dc, 2 sl st in ch-1 sp, sl st in dc = corner] in corner group, sl st to next corner, make corner, sl st to color change, drop first color, pick up next color, rep from * to end of rnd, join to first sl st. Fasten off.

labyrinth

It is said that walking a labyrinth can help to calm your soul. When walking is not possible, a finger labyrinth, placed on your lap, is the next best thing to experiencing the benefits of a meditation on foot. This design, meant to hang on the wall when it's not being used as a finger labyrinth, is a replica of a prototype found in a Roman villa in first century Italy.

skill level

Intermediate

size

20.5" x 22.5"

materials

 Worsted Weight Yarn (4 ounces/190 yards, 114 grams/174 meters per skein):

Orchid (A) – 1 skein

 Bulky Weight Yarn (1.75 ounces/77 yards, 50 grams/70 meters per skein):

White (B) – 2 skeins

• Crochet hook, size H/8 (5 mm) or size needed to obtain gauge
• Rug liner: ⅔ yard (minimum of 54 squares wide)
• Masonite 20" x 22" piece
• Large self-leveling sawtooth picture hanger with nails
• Wood, three (3" x 3⅜" x ¾") pieces
• Hammer
• White glue
• White primer spray paint
• Photo mount spray adhesive
• Wax paper, two 25" lengths
• Tapestry needle to work in ends

gauge

10 squares = approx 4" one way x 4½" the other way

notes

1. Cut rug liner to 54 squares by 54 squares. The design itself is 44 squares by 44 squares with a 4-row border (1 row is folded under to finish off edges). Leave 5 squares unworked around outside edges of labyrinth to be filled in with trim.
2. Although it looks like it, the rug liner is NOT square.

instructions for dragon curves

Following Chart A on page 32, begin at any desired point. Attach A with a sc on first leg, sc on same leg, 2 sc on next leg, cont in this pattern for entire project, finish off, work in ends. When paths intersect, attach ending sc of new path to side of old path.

Chart A

red = orchid labyrinth
blue = white background

Chart B

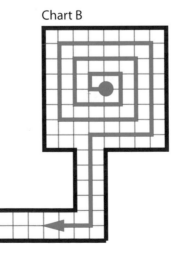

notes

1. When turning a corner, double check to make sure you are in the right lane; it's easy to drift into another lane. Check often! Suggestion: Do not cut yarn at end of path until you double-check your work.

2. One lane remains between all legs of the design.

trim

inside/outside labyrinth

Rnd 1: Following Chart B, attach B with a sc at center of labyrinth and work your way out through the entire pathway, placing 1 sc on each leg. When you get to the entrance, turn a corner and cont, following the outline of the labyrinth around to the front again, sl st to first sc outside of labyrinth. Fasten off.

outside labyrinth

Note: Always work in the same direction.

Rnd 2: Join anywhere with a sc and sc around, following the outline of the labyrinth, sl st to beg sc. Fasten off.

Rnd 3: Fold the outside edge under 1 rnd, join anywhere with a sc and, working through the third and fifth rnds at the same time, sc around, sl st to beg sc. Fasten off. This puts rnd 4 on the outside of the piece.

Rnd 4: Join anywhere with a sc, sc on each leg around, placing 2 sc in each corner. Fasten off — 52 sc on each side.

mounting

This is worth repeating: The rug liner is NOT square, although it looks like it. So plan ahead before mounting the work to the board. Determine which side is the top of your wall hanging and orient the masonite accordingly. Nail picture hanger to one of the pieces of wood. Glue to center back of masonite ¾" down from the top. Glue other 2 pieces in the bottom corners on the back of the masonite ¾" up from the bottom and ¾" in from the sides. Let dry 30 minutes. Spray paint front and sides of masonite, following directions on the can. Rep as necessary. Let dry overnight. Spray a double coat of adhesive to back of wall hanging and front of masonite, following directions on the can. Let set 2-3 minutes. (**Note:** The remainder of the mounting will go more smoothly if two people are involved.) Lay wax paper sheets side by side vertically on masonite, leaving 2" of masonite exposed at the top. Visually position hanging where you think you want it to be, then press the top 2" of the hanging to the exposed masonite. The wax paper acts as a release paper, preventing the remainder of the hanging from sticking to the masonite until you are ready. Pull wax paper down in 2" increments as the hanging makes contact with the masonite, smoothing and stretching the hanging as you go. When finished, press down firmly over entire surface. Let dry overnight.

Hang the labyrinth on the wall and step back to admire your work. When ready to meditate, place it on your lap and let your fingers take the lead. It is said that on the journey in, one cleanses the soul. On the journey out, one is born anew.

dragon curve challenges

prologue

Everything you need to know (well, at least for this book) about working with dragon curves.

1. The head (start) and tail (finish) can begin and end anywhere you like (such as on the scarf), or they can be joined to make an enclosed shape (like the afghan flowers).

2. Dragon curves can accommodate any design. You may want to chart it out in advance, or you may prefer to work freely and see where you end up. Whichever way you choose, go for it! Let the creativity begin!

3. If charting, plan the background grid in advance, so it is the right size to accommodate your design. Graph paper makes this job easy.

4. Because there is an upright stitch at each end of each row or round, there is always one more upright stitch than chain spaces on a background grid. (For example, 28 stitches = 10 dc and 9 ch-2 spaces.)

5. The foundation row of the background grid is always included in the row count. So if you need an even number of rows for a balanced design, the total row count must be uneven.

6. The grid can be made with sc, dc, or tr, depending on your design. To keep the grid square, ch 1 and sk 1 stitch between scs, ch 2 and sk 2 between dcs, and ch 3 and sk 3 between trs.

7. The larger the grid, the more stitches you'll need on each side for the vertical and horizontal movements of the dragon curve. For example: sc = 2 or 3, dc = 3 or 4, tr = 4 or 5, depending on the effect you want. Keep in mind that more than 2 sc, 3 dc or 4 tr will distort your fabric (the scarf is an example of intentional distortion). You can also work sc dragon curves on a dc grid or vice versa, if you adjust the number of stitches accordingly.

8. Any crochet stitch will make an attractive dragon curve; the taller the stitch, the more prominent it becomes in the design. Try more than one stitch height for an interesting look. How about adding stitches on top of stitches? It just depends on the look you want.

9. These projects are just a starting point. They are an invitation to experiment and be creative in any direction you choose.

dragon curve design challenges

1. Make a mesh scarf like the one on page 12 and cover it from end to end with dragon curves — either one long dragon or several small ones in different colors. To keep it light and supple, use very fine yarn and work the base with the thread doubled. Then use a

level 3

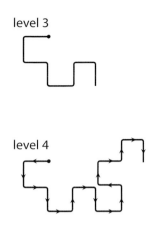

level 4

level 5

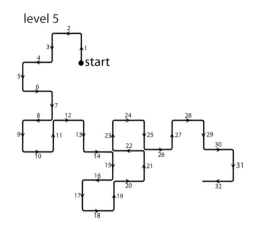

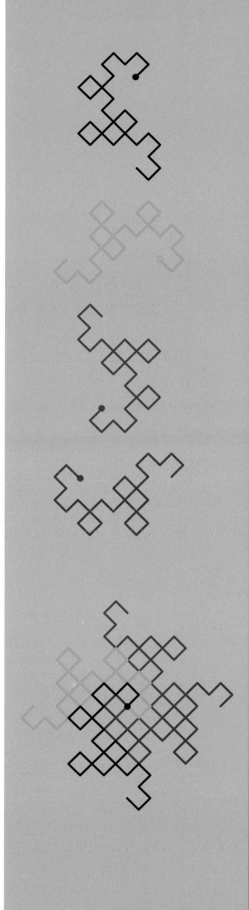

single strand for the dragon curve embellishment. And no one says you're limited to just going back and forth.

2. Using the doormat charts on page 25, make a bathmat with three or more colors.

3. Fashion an 8" square purse similar to the Craft Tote on page 18, but create your own design and use as fine a thread as you're comfortable working with and an appropriately sized hook. Substitute purchased handles or silken cords for the hollow tubing. Tassels are wonderful additions to corners.

4. Find an 18" decorator pillow to complement your yarns and design a two-sided floor pillow to match the afghan on page 26: blue with orange dragon curves on one side, orange with blue dragon curves on the other. Alter the stitch counts to accommodate the different shape and size.

5. Create a 16" x 50" rectangle with a triple crochet mesh like the shawl on page 14, and embellish it with your own versions of dragon curves. Leave as is for a shawl, or sew the long sides together for 6" or so and create a shrug. (Foundation row starts with a tr in the eleventh chain from the hook, chain seven to turn).

6. How about a round project? How could you incorporate dragon curves into a round shape?

7. Make another shawl like the one on page 14, but this time dream up your own surface design using the level 3 and 4 dragon curves above.

8. At right is a set of four level 5 dragon curves joined tail to tail. What can you do with them? How about a free form rug with these curves in the center, surrounded by swirls or spirals?

chapter 2

golden

ratio

golden ratio

The golden ratio came to be called that because early mathematicians, architects and artists thought the most beautiful way to divide up spaces was with ⅔–⅓ proportions. Of course, they weren't thinking in such simplistic terms, they had a specific name and number in mind.

Technically, it is called phi Φ (pronounced "fee"), and it looks like this: .61803. It's also called Phi (with a capital P) and it looks like this: 1.6180339887. For ease of use throughout the book, both numbers are rounded up to the nearest whole number and become .62 and 1.62.

The name comes from Phidias, a distinguished Greek sculptor, who lived around 490 to 430 BC and who frequently made deliberate use of the golden ratio in his art.

As we divide spaces into golden segments for the projects, we'll be relying on three numbers.

1. To get the next largest number, multiply by 1.62. Let's say we're making a pattern for a rug that will be 20" wide. To find the correct proportion for the length, multiply 20" x 1.62 = 32". Thus our rug will be a 20" x 32" golden rectangle.

2. For the next smallest number, multiply by .62. Suppose we want a rug that's 20" long. To find the width, multiply 20" x .62 = 12". The perfectly proportioned rug will measure 12" x 20".

3. And any space that's divided into two golden segments will be proportioned 38% and 62%.

The interesting thing about Phi/phi is that it's the only mathematical formula where, if you make a golden cut in a golden rectangle, the .62 becomes a square and the remaining .38 becomes another golden rectangle.

To use our 20" x 32" rug as a model, 32" x .62 = 20", and 32" x .38 = 12". The golden cut falls at 20", creating a 20" square, with a rectangle left over that now measures 12" x 20", another perfect golden rectangle.

This can be repeated over and over again, as the drawing on the opposite page illustrates.

A golden ratio is not limited to rectangles. It can be used with any geometric figure. In this chapter there are three shapes used for the six projects: two squares, three rectangles, and a star. The 7-pointed star is included to demonstrate the versatility of what's been called "the world's most astonishing number."

Interpreted for crochet, use of the golden ratio is determined by three things: stitch count, row count, and row and stitch counts. In this chapter there is one project determined by stitch count (puzzle placemat) two based on

row count (scarf and afghan), and three governed by both row and stitch counts (wall hanging, flower pillow, and poncho).

To learn more about the golden ratio, check out the websites and books in the Resources section in the back of the book. And take a look at the more advanced projects in the Challenges section on page 67.

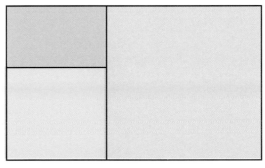

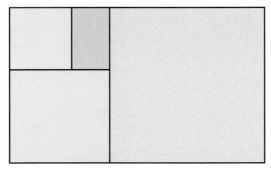

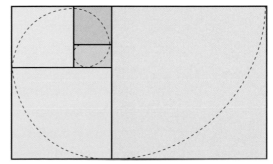

golden scarf

Counting stitches determines the width of this scarf, and counting rows dictates the length. These are very simple ways to create interesting and unique designs that you can proudly claim as your own.

skill level:

Easy

size

5" x 46" (excluding fringe)

materials

 Worsted Weight Yarn (3.5 ounces/200 yards, 100 grams/183 meters per skein):

Variegated Gray (A) – 1 skein
Blue (B) – 1 skein
• Crochet hooks, size H/8 (5 mm) and I/9 (5.5 mm)
• Tapestry needle to work in ends

gauge

9 esc and 7 rows = 3"

notes

1. The width becomes a golden ratio by dividing stitches (10 of color A and 5 of color B, or .62 and .38). The length is divided into golden segments of 16 and 26 rows (16 x 1.62 = 26). This was easily turned into a palindrome sequence of 16-26-16-26-16 of color A, with each segment separated by 3 rows of color B.

2. To change colors, see notes on page 104.

3. Always drop unused yarn to WS of work.

special stitch

Extended single crochet (esc): Insert hook into next st, yo and pull through, yo and pull through 1 lp, yo and pull through rem 2 lps.

instructions

Note: When changing colors within the body of the scarf, cut yarn, leaving a 6" tail to weave in.

Foundation Row: With A and smaller hook, ch 10, drop A, pick up B, ch 6. Turn — 16 ch.

Row 1: Esc in second ch from hook and next 4 ch, drop B, pick up A, esc in last l0 ch. Turn — 15 esc.

Row 2: With A, ch 1, esc in first 10 esc, drop A, pick up B, esc in last 5 esc. Turn.

Row 3: With B, ch 1, esc in first 5 esc, drop B, pick up A, esc in last

10 esc. Turn.

Row 4: Rep row 2.

Rows 5–16: Rep rows 3 and 2, cut yarn. Turn.

Rows 17–19: With B and larger hook, ch 1, sc in each st across. Turn.

Rows 20–45: With smaller hook and reverse color placement, rep rows 3 and 2 thirteen times.

Rows 46–48: Rep rows 17–19.

Rows 49–64: Rep rows 3 and 2 eight times.

Rows 65–112: Rep rows 17–64. Fasten off.

edging

With A and smaller hook, place eight fringes evenly spaced across 15 sts as follows:

Sl st in first st, ch 16, going under top strand only, sl st in second ch from hook and each ch to end (15 sl sts); *sl st in next 2 sts, ch and sl st designated amounts (see chart below), rep from * to end, sl st in same st as last fringe.

Fasten off.

Ch 16 — 15 sl st, one time.
Ch 21— 20 sl st, two times.
Ch 26 — 25 sl st, two times.
Ch 21— 20 sl st, two times.
Ch 16 — 15 sl st, one time.
Rep on other end.

16	26	16	26	16
.38	.62	.38	.62	.38

golden ratio divided into golden sections based on number of rows

summer wall hanging

Often, crochet means making something practical: beautiful, but practical. There are moments, though, when practical must step aside because you are simply feeling creative. That's what this project is all about. Have fun with it.

skill level

Easy

size

14" x 22" (2 golden rectangles!)

materials

 Worsted Weight Yarn (4 ounces/190 yards, 114 grams/174 meters per skein):
Yellow (A) – 2 skeins
Orange (B) – 1 skein
• Crochet hooks, sizes H/8 (5 mm) and I/9 (5.5 mm)
• Two – 18" lengths of rigid hollow plastic tubing, ½" outside diameter/¼" inside diameter (see Resources on page 111)
• Yarn and beads for hanging and embellishment (E):
2 yards – ⅛" yellow cord (available at fabric stores) (EA), 17 yards – bulky weight yarn (EB), 15 yards – yellow worsted weight yarn (EC)
• Wire wrapped beads
• Hook or wire for threading yarn through tubing
• Tapestry needle to work in ends

gauge

10 sts = 3" and 12 rows = 3½"

note

1. Larger hook is used on Foundation Rows and Rows 1 and 78 only.

instructions
yellow section

Foundation Row: With larger hook and A, ch 36.
Row 1 (RS): Sl st in second ch from hook and each ch to end. Turn — 35 sl st.
Row 2: With smaller hook ch 5 (counts as first dtr), dtr in back lp of each sl st to end. Turn.
Row 3: With smaller hook, ch 1, with sc join back lp of each dtr to front lp of sl st in row below (Row 1), ending in top of tch. Turn.

First Spiral Strip
Rows 4–25: Ch 1, sc in 5 sc. Turn. At the end of row 25, fasten off.

**Second Through Seventh
Spiral Strips**

Row 4: Reattach with sc in next sc
on row 3, sc in next 4 sc. Turn.

Rows 5–25: Ch 1, sc in 5 sc. Turn.
At the end of row 25, fasten off.
Rep for each of rem 5 spirals.

Row 26 (RS): Twist first strip a
half turn. Sc in each sc — 5 sc.
Join rem 6 strips, twisting each
strip a half turn before working 1
sc in each sc. Turn — 35 sts.

Rows 27–28: Ch 1, sc across.
Turn.

Rows 29 (WS)–53: Rep rows
4–28 for all spirals.

Rows 54 (WS)–75: Rep rows
4–25 for all spirals.

Row 76 (RS): Rep row 26.
Turn.

Row 77: Ch 5 (counts as first dtr),
dtr in back lp of each sc across.
Turn.

Row 78: With larger hook, ch 1.
Using sl st, join back lp of dtr and
front lp of sl st in row below, ending in top of tch. Fasten off.

orange section

Foundation Row: With larger
hook, ch 21.

Row 1 (RS): Sl st in second ch
from hook and each ch to end.
Turn — 20 sl st.

Row 2: With smaller hook, ch 4
(counts as first dtr), dtr in back lp
of each sl st to end. Turn.

Row 3: With smaller hook, ch 1.
With sc, join back lp of each dtr

and front lp of sl st in row below,
ending in top of tch. Turn.

First Spiral Strip

Rows 4–25: Ch 1, sc in first 5 sc.
Turn. At the end of row 25,
fasten off.

Second Through Fourth Spiral
Strips

Row 4: Reattach with sc in next sc
on row 3, sc in next 4 sc. Turn.

Rows 5–25: Ch 1, sc in 5 sc. Turn.
At the end of row 25, fasten off.
Rep for last two strips.

Row 26 (RS): Twist first strip a half
turn. Sc in each sc — 5 sc. Twist
each rem strip once before rejoin-
ing; sc in each sc. Turn — 20 sc.

Rows 27–28: Ch 1, sc across. Turn.

Rows 29 (WS)–53: Rep rows 4–28 for all spirals.

Rows 54 (WS)–75: Rep rows 4–25 for all spirals.

Row 76 (RS): Rep row 26. Turn.

Row 77: Ch 5 (counts as first dtr), dtr in back lp of each sc across. Turn.

Row 78: With larger hook, ch 1. Using sl st, join back lp of each dtr to front lp of sl st in row below, ending in top of tch. Fasten off.

top tubing/hanger

Note: Refer to list of materials for explanation of EA, EB, and EC.

1. Using row of dtr as casing at top of hanging, insert plastic tubing into top casings of gold and orange pieces.

2. Thread EA, two 85" pieces of EB, and one 85" piece of EC through top tubing. Omitting EC, tie EA and EB in a square knot in the center as desired to make the hanger. (See page 21 for how to tie a square knot.)

3. Wrap EA and EB tog around hanger 7 times, ending up at each end of tubing. Drop EA.

4. With EB and EC, tie a knot at each end of tubing. Then tie an overhand knot next to original knot at end of tubing, but leave loop open.

5. For each tassel, cut five 16-inch strands each of EB and EC.

6. Thread tassel pieces halfway through open loop, along with the end of EA.

7. Close loop by pulling firmly on EB and EC ends.

8. Wrap ends of EB and EC for about ½" around top of tassel pieces and the end of EA.

9. Thread ends of EB and EC individually onto tapestry needle, insert needle from top to bottom under wrapped ends at back of tassel and pull through.

10. Cut end of EA off even with bottom of wrapping.

Rep steps 6–10 for other side. Trim tassel ends evenly.

bottom tubing

1. Using row of dtr as casing at bottom of hanging, insert tubing into bottom casings of gold and orange pieces.

2. Thread three 40-inch pieces of EB and three 40-inch pieces of EC through bottom tubing.

3–5. Rep steps 4–6 of top tubing.

6. Thread 3 of the 6 ends from the tubing, along with the tassel pieces, through open loop of overhand knot.

7–9. Rep steps 8–10 of top tubing, ignoring any reference to EA. Trim tassel ends evenly.

bead embellishments

Choose as many beads as desired and, matching yarn colors, randomly sew them onto RS of wall hanging, weaving in ends on WS.

Beads used for this project:
Bead Heaven (Halcraft USA) wire wrapped beads 10 per package: #6792 Ruby, #67283 Festival

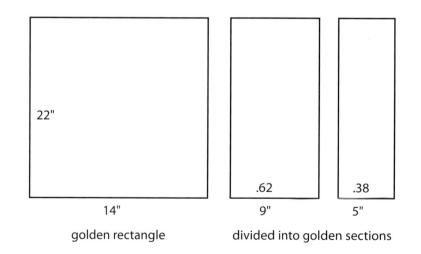

golden rectangle   divided into golden sections

star
afghan

Seven has long been considered a lucky or magical number. It is also the number of the world's ancient wonders, the seven visible colors of the rainbow, the seven tones of the musical scale, and the number of different levels of Heaven. A seven-pointed star afghan seemed like the perfect project to demonstrate that the golden ratio can be used with any shape.

skill level

■■□□ Easy

size

58" from point to point

materials

2 FINE Worsted Weight Yarn: (4 ounces/190 yards. 114 grams/ 174 meters per skein):

Orchid (A) – 7 skeins
Dark purple (B) – 5 skeins
• Crochet hook, size J/10/6mm
• Tapestry needle to work in ends

gauge

6 FPdc = 2", 4 rounds = 1½"

notes

1. At this gauge, a 40-row palindrome pattern of 11-7-4-7-11 makes a 58" diameter afghan, a good size for a snooze.

2. At the end of rounds 11, 18, 22 and 29, sl st in back lp of first FPdc and fasten off old color. At the beg of rounds 12, 19, 23 and 30, join new color with a sl st in the front lp of the same st, ch 3 and proceed in established pattern.

special stitches

Front Post dc (FPdc): Yo, insert hook from front-to-back-to-front around post of designated stitch, yo, pull through and complete like a regular dc.

Color Sequence: Rnds 1–11, A; 12–18, B; 19–22, A; 23–29, B; 30–40, A.

instructions

Foundation Rnd: With A, ch 4, join with sl st to first ch.

Rnd 1: Ch 6, dc in ring, (ch 3, dc in ring) 5 times; ch 3, sl st to third ch of beg ch-6 — 7 ch-3 sps.

Rnd 2: Ch 3 (counts as first dc throughout), (dc, ch 2, 2 dc) in first ch-3 sp, [2 dc, ch 2, 2 dc = point] in rem 6 ch-3 sps; sl st to top of beg ch-3.

Rnd 3: Ch 3, FPdc around first dc, point in next ch-2 sp, *[FPdc around next dc, sk 2 dc, FPdc around next dc = inner angle], point in next ch-2 sp, rep from * around; FPdc around next dc, sk beg ch-3 and sl st to top of beg FPdc.

Rnd 4: Ch 3, FPdc around next 2 dc, point in ch-2 sp; *FPdc around next 2 dc, inner angle, FPdc around next 2 dc, point in ch-2 sp, rep from * around; FPdc around next 2 dc, sk beg ch-3 and sl st to top of beg FPdc.

Rnd 5: Ch 3, FPdc around next 3 sts, point in ch-2 sp, *FPdc around next 3 sts, inner angle, FPdc around next 3 sts, point in ch-2 sp, rep from * around; FPdc around next 3 sts, sk beg ch-3 and sl st to top of beg FPdc.

Rnds 6–40: Cont in pattern, increasing 1 FPdc on each side of each point on each rnd, skipping 2 dc at each inner angle — 38 sts on each side of each point at the end of rnd 40.

edging

Rnd 1: With B, join with a sc in same sl st as join, 39 sc up side to point, (2 sc, ch 2, 2 sc) in ch-2 sp, 40 sc down side to inner angle, *40 sc up side to point, (2 sc, ch 2, 2 sc) in ch-2 sp, 40 sc down side to inner angle, rep from * around, join to first sc with sl st — 602 sc.

Rnd 2: Ch 1, sc in same sc as join, 41 sc up side to point, 3 sc in ch-2 sp, 42 sc down to inner angle, *42 sc up side to point, 3 sc in ch-2 sp, 42 sc down to inner angle, rep from * around; join to first sc with sl st — 609 sc.

Rnd 3: Ch 1 (counts as first sl st), sk first sc, sl st in each st around, join to beg ch-1. Fasten off.

flower power pillow

What I like about golden ratios is that they're flexible. Once the proportions are established you are free to experiment with decorative variations. Take this pillow, for example. The guidelines are clear; separate a square shape into golden sections. But after that, do whatever you want in each of the three areas. I chose to put flowers in all of mine, but I could just as easily have substituted bobbles and stripes in two of them.

skill level

Easy

size

17" x 17" (to fit 18" pillow form)

materials

 Worsted Weight Yarn (4 ounces/190 yards, 114 grams/174 meters per skein):

Purple (A) – 4 skeins
Orange (B) – 1 skein
Green (C) – 2 skeins
• 18" pillow form
• Crochet hooks, sizes H/8 (5 mm) and G/6 (4 mm)
• Tapestry needle to work in ends

gauge

8 hdc and 5 rows = 2"

notes

1. Even rows, work in back loops only; odd rows, work in front loops only.
2. To change colors, see notes on page 104.
3. Chart is marked for RHC and LHC.

special stitches

FORKED CLUSTER (FC)
First FC st of Row: Ch 3 (counts as dc), yo, insert hook into first st, yo and pull through, yo, insert hook into next st, yo and pull through (5 lps on hook), [yo and pull through 3 lps] twice.

FC subsequent sts: Yo, insert hook into same st as previous FC, yo and pull through, yo, insert hook into next st, yo and pull through, [yo and pull through 3 lps] twice.

FC corner: FC through to last sc before corner sc, ch 1, FC in same sc and corner sc, ch 1, FC in corner sc, ch 1, FC in corner sc and next sc, ch 1, proceed in pattern st to end, sl st to top of beg ch-3.

instructions

PILLOW FRONT
Foundation Row: With larger hook and A, ch 67.
Row 1 (WS): Hdc in third ch from hook, and following chart, hdc in each ch across. Turn — 65 hdc.
Row 2 and all even rows: Ch 1 (does not count as a st), working

in back lps, follow chart and hdc in each hdc across. Turn.

Row 3 and all odd rows: Ch 1 (does not count as a st), working in front lps, follow chart and hdc in each hdc across. Turn.

Rep rows 2 and 3 for 40 rows, ending with row 2. Fasten off.

edging

With A and WS facing, sc evenly around, placing 3 sc in each corner st — 65 sc between corner sc on all 4 sides. Fasten off.

flowers

Refer to chart. Working with smaller hook in free lps on designated rows, join with sl st, very loosely *ch 5, working in top lps only, 12 sc in second ch from hook, 3 sc in each of third, fourth and fifth chs, sl st in sixth, sev-enth and eighth chs, sl st in next 3 chs on pillow. Rep from * for 17 rows of 10 flowers for A, 4 rows of 5 flowers for B, and 10 rows of five flowers for C.

tossed salad pillow back

The photographed model is the result of tying together 3 different lengths of yarn. It results in a truly random look and many knots to poke through to the wrong side. To cut down on the number of knots, and for a different look, make the yarn strands longer. You can also make your own self-striping yarn by cutting the yarn into 6-yard lengths for 1 row, 12 yards for 2 rows, etc.

Magic ball of yarn: Take about 2 ounces each of A, B, and C and cut into 90 12-inch lengths, 120 30-inch lengths, and 105 50-inch lengths. Put in a pile and toss all strands together as if making a salad. Pick them up at random and tie ends together in a secure knot. As you go along, wind the yarn loosely into a ball. You have just made a magic ball — your own variegated yarn, a perfect match for the solid colors on the front of the pillow.

Foundation Row: Ch 67.
Note: Because the yarn is altered, the back requires 2 more rows to equal 17".
Rows 1–42: Follow the stitch pattern of hdc in front or back loops, as for the Pillow Front. As you're crocheting, the knots will appear on both sides of the fabric. When finished, poke all knots through to WS of work. From time to

time a knot will distort a stitch, making it easy to overlook on the next row. Count your stitches at regular intervals.

edging

Rep edging for Pillow Front.

joining front and back

Rnd 1: With WS tog, join Front and Back with a sc through both sides, placing 3 sc in each corner sc, sl st to beg sc. When three sides are joined, insert pillow form and then complete joining.

Rnd 2: Referring to Special Stitch section, FC around entire pillow. Fasten off.

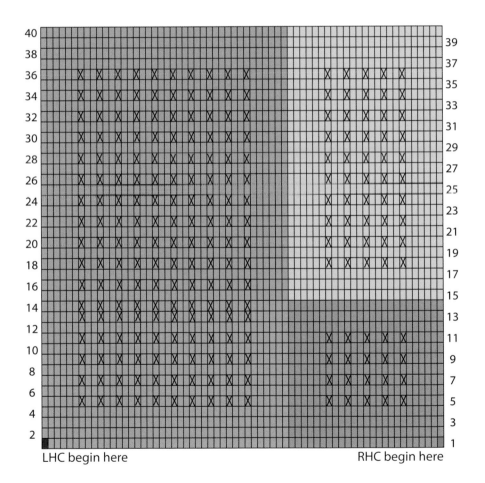

LHC begin here   RHC begin here

puzzle placemats

The basic pattern is a simple 6" square that has been divided into two .62/.38 ratios. The placemats consist of six squares, with the squares arranged differently for each one. To give your table a festive look, find some complementary cotton fabric and make a tablecloth and napkins to match.

skill level

Easy

size

Approx 12" x 18" (before edging)

materials

 Worsted Weight Yarn (2.50 ounces/120 yards, 70 grams/109 meters per ball):

Blue (A) – 4 balls
Lime (B) – 3 balls
Pink 3(C) – 2 balls
• Crochet hooks, size G/6 (4 mm) and F/5 (3.75 mm)
• Tapestry needle to work in ends

gauge

One design unit = 6" square

notes

1. There are two ways to make these placemats. Make six separate squares for each, arrange them using the suggested arrangements or design your own, then sew them together. But if, like me, you'd rather not sew the squares together, follow the charts and make each placemat in one continuous piece.

2. If I made the basic block strictly by the golden ratio rule, it should have been 24 stitches by 18 rows. But I needed one more row to get the 6" height, so the block ended up 24 stitches by 19 rows. With 19 rows, the proper proportions should have been 5 rows of pink, 7 of lime and 7 of blue, but the color intensities made a more pleasing visual balance with a 5-8-6 sequence.

3. Because they are small, I used a separate ball of yarn for each color change. If you prefer to use bobbins, you'll need 7 feet for each block of pink and 12 yards for each block of lime.

4. To change colors, see notes on page 104.

5. With the exception of row 1, the entire placemat is worked in the front loop only of each sc.

6. Charts are marked for RHC and LHC.

Placemat # 1

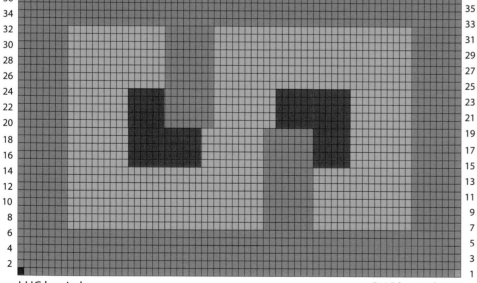

LHC begin here   RHC begin here

Basic Block

instructions

Basic Block:

With A, using smaller crochet hook, ch 25.

Row 1: Sc in second ch from hook and each ch across. Turn — 24 sc.

Row 2: Ch 1, sc in front lp of each sc across. Turn.

Rows 3-6: Rep row 2.

Rows 7-19: Follow chart.

Placemat # 2

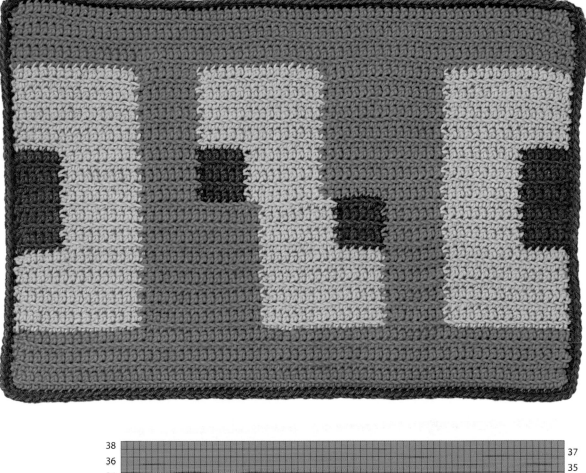

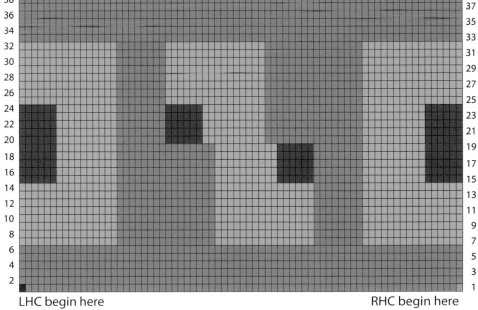

LHC begin here   RHC begin here

placemats 1–4

Foundation Row: With larger hook and A, ch 73.

Row 1 (RS): With smaller hook, sc in second ch from hook and each ch across. Turn — 72 sc.

Row 2: Ch 1, sc in front lp of each sc across. Turn.

Rows 3-6: Rep row 2.

Rows 7-32: Follow charts.

Rows 33-38: Rep row 2. Fasten off.

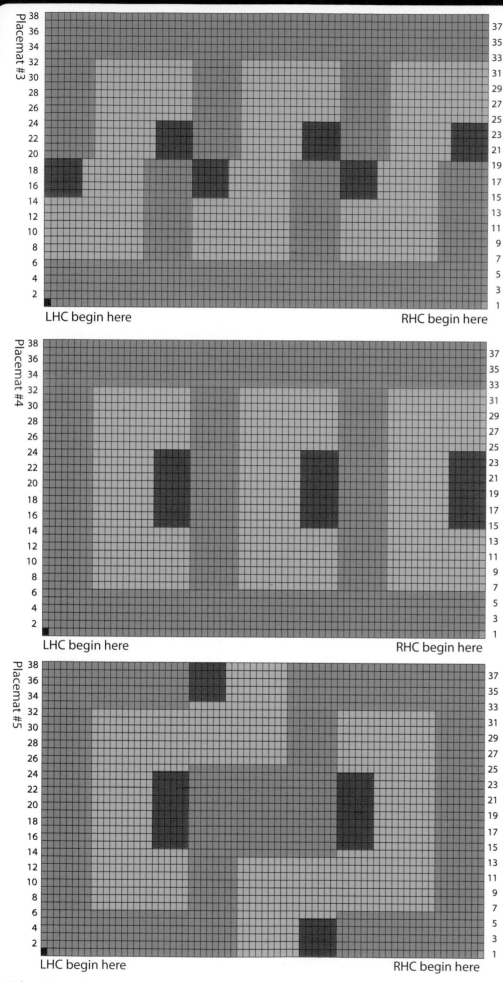

Placemat #3

38
36
34
32
30
28
26
24
22
20
18
16
14
12
10
8
6
4
2

37
35
33
31
29
27
25
23
21
19
17
15
13
11
9
7
5
3
1

LHC begin here

RHC begin here

Placemat #4

38
36
34
32
30
28
26
24
22
20
18
16
14
12
10
8
6
4
2

37
35
33
31
29
27
25
23
21
19
17
15
13
11
9
7
5
3
1

LHC begin here

RHC begin here

Placemat #5

38
36
34
32
30
28
26
24
22
20
18
16
14
12
10
8
6
4
2

37
35
33
31
29
27
25
23
21
19
17
15
13
11
9
7
5
3
1

LHC begin here

RHC begin here

edging

Rnd 1 (RS): With smaller hook and C, join with sc in any st and sc evenly around, placing 3 sc in each corner st, join with sl st in front lp of beg sc.

Rnd 2: Ch 1 (counts as first sl st), sk first sc, sl st in front loop of each sc around, join with sl st in beg ch-1. Fasten off.

placemats 5–8

Foundation Row: With larger hook and A, ch 73.

Row 1: With smaller hook, sc in second ch from hook, and following chart, sc in each ch across. Turn — 72 sc.

Rows 2–38: Ch 1 and following chart, sc in front lp of each sc across.

Fasten off at the end of row 38.

edging

Follow instructions for placemats 1–4.

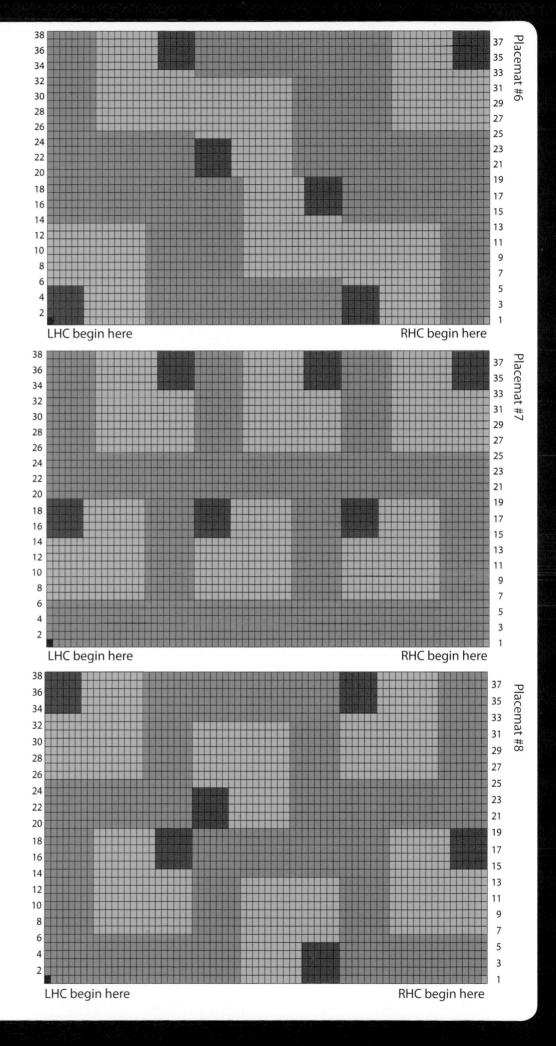

LHC begin here   RHC begin here

LHC begin here   RHC begin here

LHC begin here   RHC begin here

garden poncho

This pattern demonstrates two different ways to use the same space within a golden rectangle. One side is divided into golden proportions vertically, the other side horizontally. Within the divisions the patterns follow no mathematical formula. I just experimented with a computer program until I was pleased with the results. Graph paper and colored pencils would also work.

skill level

■ ■ □ □
Easy

size**

18" x 29" (20" x 31" with 1" edging)

materials

 Worsted Weight Yarn (3.5 ounces/245 yards, 100 grams/ 225 meters per skein):
Dark Green (A) – 2 skeins
Orange (B) – 1 skein)
Medium Green (C) – 2 skeins
Light Green (D) – 1 skein
• Crochet hook, sizes J/10 (6 mm) and I/9 (5.5 mm) or size needed to obtain gauge
• Stitch markers
• Tapestry needle to work in ends

gauge

9 hdc = 2.5", 9 rows = 4"

**To make a larger size
First method: Decide how long you want it to be and multiply by 1.62 to get the width (ex: 22" x 1.62 = 36" yields a finished size of 22" x 36").

Second method (same results): Decide how wide you want it to be and multiply by .62 to get the length (ex: 36" x .62 = 22" yields a finished size of 36" x 22").
Both methods: Then use .62 and .38 to divide up the interior spaces (for horizontal design: 22" x .62 = 14" and 22" x .38 = 8"; 14" + 8" = 22") and (for vertical design: 36" x .62 = 22" and 36" x .38 = 14"; 22" + 14" = 36").
Then choose the stitch and hook size you want to use, make a swatch, and work out your stitch and row counts from there. Remember to also increase the amount of yarn to use.
Note: Both sides of my poncho are really three golden rectangles in one (see drawings on page 63).

notes

1. Chain 1 to turn all rows.
2. When edging long sides, mark-

ers placed at regular intervals will help you keep track of your stitch count.

3. To change colors see notes on page 104.

pattern stitch

*Hdc in back lp of first hdc, hdc in front lp of next hdc, rep from * across. Turn.

instructions

SIDE 1

Foundation Row: With larger hook and A, ch 70.

Row 1: Hdc in third ch from hook and, following chart A, hdc in each ch across, turn — 68 hdc.

Rows 2–69: Ch 1 (does not count as a st) and, working in pattern st, cont to follow chart A on page 64. Fasten off at end of row 69.

SIDE 2

Same as Side 1, except follow chart B.

edging (both sides)

Rnd 1 (RS): Matching colors, with smaller hook attach with a sc and sc evenly around, placing 3 sc in each corner, sl st to beg sc. Turn — 68 sts between corner scs on short side, 106 sc between corner scs on long sides.

Rnd 2: Ch 1 and sc evenly around, placing 3 sc in each corner sc, sl st to beg sc, fasten off — 70 sc between corner scs on short sides, 108 sc between corner scs on long sides.

seams

Notes for all seams:

1. Hold pieces with RS facing each other, and you are working on the WS.

2. Work through back lp of closest side and front lp of other side.

shoulders

Using smaller hook and matching colors, attach with a sl st in corner sc, sl st in next 41 sc. Fasten off. Skip 26 sc for neck opening. Attach with a sl st in next sc, sl st in last 41 sc, ending in corner sc, fasten off — 84 sl sts.

sides

Using smaller hook and matching colors, attach with a sl st in corner sc, sl st in next 29 sc, fasten off — 30 sl sts.

neck opening

With smaller hook and A, work loosely joining with sl st at one shoulder seam, ch 1, (sl st, ch 1) in each sc around, sl st to beg sl st, fasten off — 52 sl sts.

Golden rectangle divided into golden segments

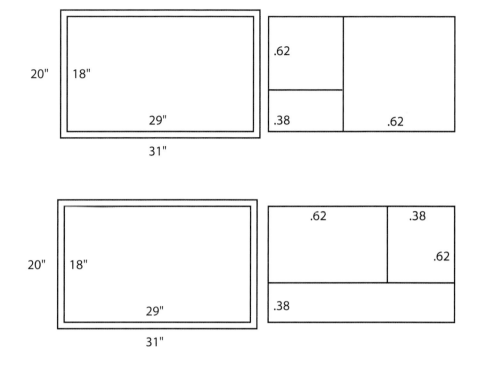

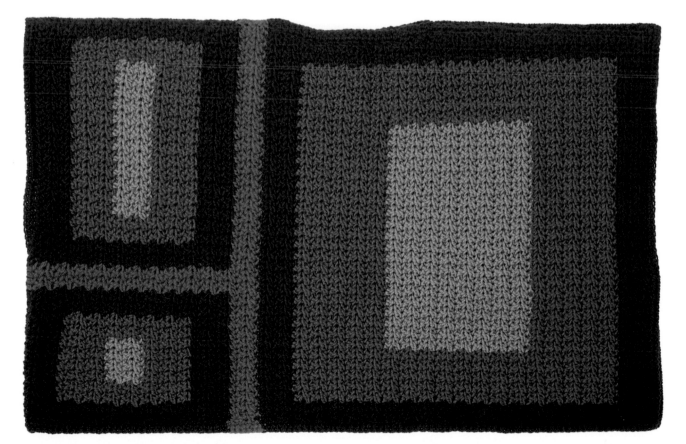

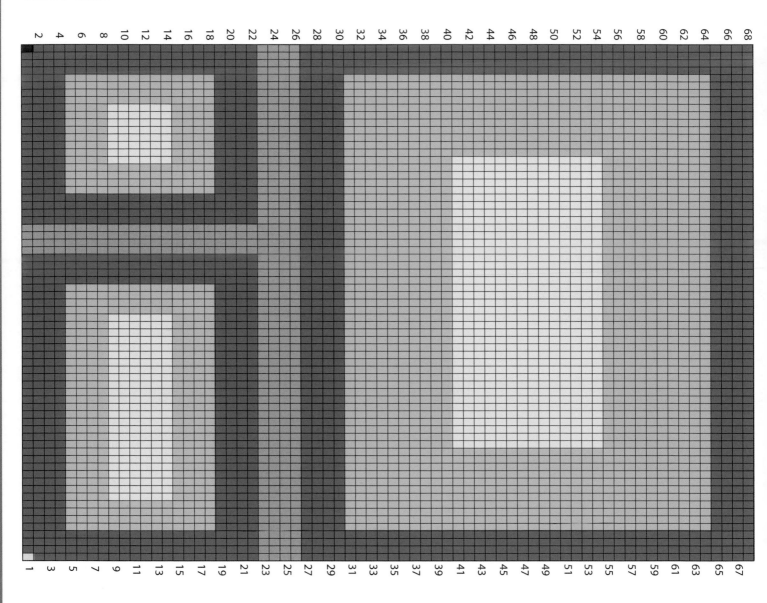

 RHC begins here

LHC begins here

Chart B – Side 2

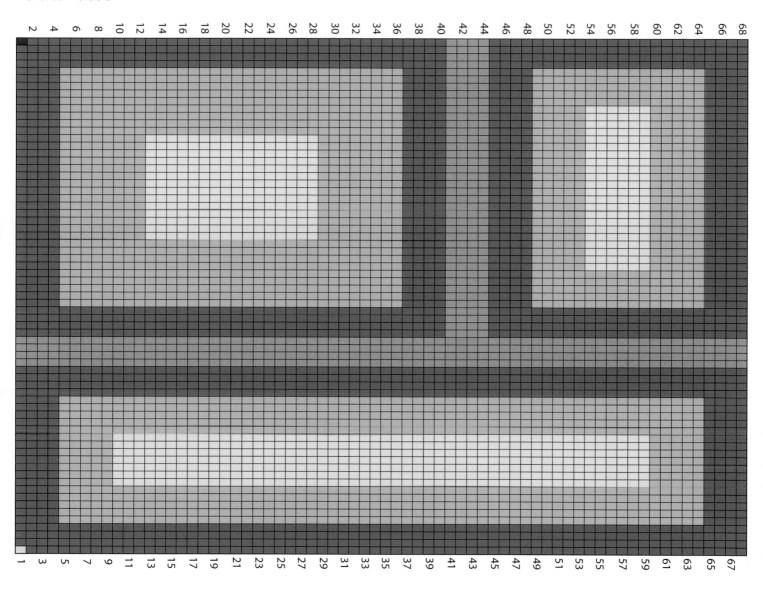

■ RHC begins here

■ LHC begins here

side notes

body measurements

The golden ratio can be your instant partner when it comes to designing clothes. Here's how it works.

1. Have someone measure you from your shoulder down to the floor.
2. Let's say the number is 45". Divide 45" into golden sections and you get: 45 x .62 = 28", and 45 x .38 = 17" (28"+ 17" = 45").
3. To interpret these numbers for crochet means that for the person who measures 45", a perfectly proportioned sweater or short jacket length would be 17", and a flattering dress or skirt or coat would be 28" long.

yarn measurements

Let's say that after making a gauge swatch, you've figured out it'll take 12 skeins of some fabulous yarn to make a project, and you want to use two colors. So, 12 x .62 = 7 and 12 x .38 = 5. You would need 7 skeins of one color and 5 skeins of another to complete the project.

Want to use a third color? 5 x .62 = 3 and 5 x .38 = 2, which means you could use 7 of color A, 3 of color B and 2 of color C for a balanced look.

It works the same with yardage. Let's say the pattern calls for 12 skeins of a yarn that comes in 210-yard skeins. 12 x 210 = 2520 yards for the entire project. Broken down proportionately, it's 2520 x .62 = 1562 yards of color A, and 2520 x .38 = 958 yards of color B. If you decide to substitute another yarn, one that comes in 190-yard skeins, for example, divide 2520 by 190 and you'll see you need 13.5 skeins of the new yarn. The proportions will remain the same because the total yardage requirement is the same.

misfit afghans or, pythagoras and fibonacci to the rescue

Suppose, after careful swatching, you've decided on a certain size, or the pattern indicates a finished measurement of 39" x 52". But after a few rows you realize that

your afghan has a mind of its own and your short side has grown to 45". Rather than rip it out, take one of these two avenues:

1. Multiply by 1.62 and come up with a new vertical dimension: 45" x 1.62 = 73".
2. Multiply by .62 and come up with a new horizontal dimension: 45" x .62 = 28".

This means that your new afghan dimensions of either 45" x 73" or 45" x 28" will be perfectly balanced, and no one but you will be the wiser!

Hopefully you have enough yarn to make these adjustments. If not, think about adding one or more colors and doing a little Fibonacci finagling (see how in the next chapter).

golden ratio challenges

1. For the placemats on pages 54-59, I came up with 8 different ways to arrange the same square. Try your hand at rearranging them by photocopying this basic square and playing with layouts. Think how you could use the concept to design a rug or an afghan. There are endless possibilities!

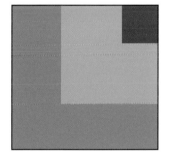

2. Using the information in the clothing side notes on the previous page, design a sweater with segments governed by 1.62 increases or .62 decreases. Stumped for what size to aim for? Use your favorite sweater as a template, then you know it'll fit.

3. Working lengthwise, design a scarf that utilizes golden proportions. Change colors both vertically and horizontally at the same time.

4. C'mon, there exists a wonderful wall hanging somewhere deep in your imagination … take the spiraling drawing in the chapter's introduction and see what you can do with it. Use a different type of yarn for each segment.

5. Design a flower pillow of your own. But instead of flowers, do something entirely different in each portion — diagonal stripes, color work circles or bumps, an uneven checkerboard. If necessary, make these separately and sew them together.

6. Take one or both of the charts for the poncho on pages 64–65 and make a wall hanging, a rug, a set of placemats, or afghans for your favorite twins.

7. Imagine a room-size rug in the shape of a 7-pointed star. Just keep going with the afghan pattern on page 46 until the points reach from wall to wall. Consider using jute, sturdy cotton yarn, or even the colored nylon cord that's sold in hardware and building supply stores.

chapter 3

fibonacci

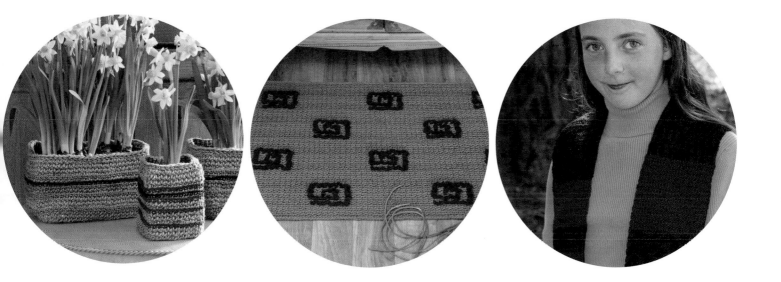

sequence

fibonacci sequence

What do daisies, pianos, pineapples, and index cards all have in common? They all illustrate the Fibonacci sequence, according to scientists and trivia buffs.

The sequence is really very simple. It starts with 0+1 and builds on itself by adding together subsequent adjacent numbers. So 0+1=1, 1+1= 2, 1+2=3, 2+3=5, and so on to a number higher than you'll ever be able to use. It looks like this when worked out 20 times:
0-1-1-2-3-5-8-13-21-34-55-89-144-233-377-610-987-1597-2584-4181-6765.

So, how do these numbers relate to daisies, pianos, pineapples, and index cards? Daisies: Most common daisies have 13, 21 or 34 petals. Pianos: Black keys appear in groups of 2 and 3; an octave has 5 black and 8 white for a total of 13 keys. Pineapples: Most pineapples have 5, 8, 13 or 21 sets of spirals of increasing steepness on their surface. Index cards: They come in two sizes, 3" x 5" and 5" x 8".

The beauty of the system is that you don't necessarily have to use the numbers in Fibonacci's sequence. Create your own! Your project can begin or end with whatever fits your needs for a particular design. Just pick a number — any number — and go from there. Just like the golden ratio, to get the next smaller number, multiply by .62. To find the next larger number, multiply by 1.62. Here's an example.

Let's say I want to incorporate the number 7 in my design. Start with 7 x .62 = 4, and 7 x 1.62 = 11. (Remember, all numbers are rounded up or down to the nearest whole number, for ease of use.) Therefore, the new sequence becomes 4-7-11, and can go up or down from there.

There's no reason to be absolutely strict about this. If a design needs customizing, bend the rules to suit your needs. Take the afghan on page 84. I wanted to work with the sequence 3-5-8 and a total of 45 rows, but I wanted to start and end each square with the same color, which required an uneven number of rows. It turned out that the numerals 3, 5, and 9 worked perfectly. So I substituted the 9 for the 8, my sequence became 3-5-9, and I got the design balance I was seeking.

Like the golden ratio, the Fibonacci sequence, interpreted for crochet, represents three different things: row or round counts, inch counts and stitch counts. In this chapter there are three projects governed by the use of row or round counts (scarf, baskets, and poncho) and four determined by the use of row or round and stitch counts (striped rug, afghan, palindrome pillows, and checkerboard rug). For an example of inch counts, check out the Challenges at the end of the chapter.

scarlet scarf

Let's start the Fibonacci journey with the basic striping sequence of 1-1-2-3-5-8-13-21 rows with tall stitches, then with short stitches in reverse order, 21-13-8-5-3-2-1-1. By reversing the sequence we create a palindrome, numbers that read the same forward and backward.

skill level

Beginner

size

4¾" x 43½" (excluding edging)

materials

Super Fine Weight Yarn (1¾ ounces/215 yards, 50 grams/197 meters per skein):
Red (A) – 1 skein
Red Variegated (B) – 1 skein
• Crochet hook, size C/2 (2.75 mm) or size needed to obtain gauge
• Tapestry needle to work in ends

gauge

Esc: 15 sts and 15 rows = 3"
Tr: 18 sts and 5 rows = 3"

notes

1. To change colors, see notes on page 104.

special stitches

Extended Single Crochet Esc: Insert hook, yo, pull yarn through, yo, pull through one loop, yo, pull through two loops.
Extended Single Crochet 2 Stitches Together Esc2tog: Insert hook, yo, pull yarn through, yo, pull through one loop, insert hook in next st, yo, pull yarn through, yo, pull through one loop, yo, pull through three loops.

instructions

Ch 30.
Row 1: With A, tr in fifth ch from hook and each ch across. Turn — 27 tr.
Row 2: With B, ch 4 (counts as first tr), sk first st, tr in each tr across, ending in top of tch. Turn.
Rows 3–4: With A, rep row 2.
Rows 5–7: With B, rep row 2.
Rows 8–12: With A, rep row 2.
Rows 13–20: With B, rep row 2.

1-1-2-3-5-8-13-21
with a tall stitch (treble crochet)

21-13-8-5-3-2-1-1
with a short stitch
(extended single crochet)

Rows 21–33: With A, rep row 2.

Rows 34–54: With B, rep row 2.

Row 55: With A, ch 1, esc in first 7 tr, esc2tog over next 2 tr, esc in next 9 tr, esc2tog over next 2 tr, esc in last 7 tr, ending in top of tch. Turn — 25 sts.

Row 56: Ch 1, esc in each esc across. Turn.

Rows 57–75: Rep row 56.

Rows 76–88: With B, rep row 56.

Rows 89–96: With A, rep row 56.

Rows 97–101: With B, rep row 56.

Rows 102–104: With A, rep row 56.

Rows 105–106: With B, rep row 56.

Row 107: With A, rep row 56.

Row 108: With B, rep row 56. Fasten off. Work in ends.

edging

On one short end, sl st in first st, *ch 8, 2 sc in second ch from hook, 2 sc in third, fourth and fifth chs, sl st in sixth, seventh and eighth chs, sl st in next two sts on scarf edge, rep from * across, end with sl st in same st as ch–8. Fasten off. Rep for other end.

striped
rug

You don't need a lot of numbers to create a handsome project. This design is a repeat of just two, 5 and 3. Remember, the numbers don't have to be Fibonacci. For example, you could use 7 and 4. Refer to the chapter introduction to create your own set of numbers.

skill level

Intermediate

size

21" x 32" (excluding fringe)

materials

Worsted Weight Yarn (3.5 oz/190 yards, 99 grams/174 meters per skein):

Light Brown (A) – 2 skeins
Gray (B) – 2 skeins

Worsted Weight Yarn (6 ounces/312 yards, 170 grams/385 meters per skein):

Brick Red (C) – 1 skein
• Crochet hook, size I/9 (5.5 mm) or size needed to obtain gauge
• Tapestry needle to work in ends

gauge

7 sts = 2"
10 rows = 3"

notes

1. Leave a 6" tail at beg and end of each row for fringe.
2. Begin each color change with the RS facing.
3. Embellishment instructions are given for both left- and right-handed crocheters.
4. To change colors, see notes on page 104.

instructions

Foundation Row: With A, ch 117. Fasten off.

Row 1 (RS): Attach A with sc in first sc, *ch 1, sk 1 ch, sc in next ch; rep from * across. Fasten off. Turn — 59 sc (58 ch-1 sps).

Row 2: Attach A with sc in first sc, *ch 1, sk 1 ch, sc in next ch; rep from * across. Fasten off. Turn.

Rows 3–4: Attach A with sc in first sc, *ch 1, sk 1 ch, sc in next ch; rep from * across. Fasten off. Turn.

Row 5 (RS): Attach A with sc in first sc, *ch 1, sk 1 ch, sc in next ch; rep from * across. Fasten off. DO NOT TURN.

Rows 6–7: Attach B with sc in first sc, *ch 1, sk 1 ch, sc in next ch; rep from * across, fasten off. Turn.

Row 8 (RS): Attach B with sc in first sc, *ch 1, sk 1 ch, sc in next ch; rep from * across. Fasten off. DO NOT TURN.

Rows 9–64: Rep rows 1–8 seven times.

Rows 65–69: Rep rows 1–5.
Last Row (RS): Attach A with sl st in first sc and sl st in each rem st across. Fasten off.
Finishing Foundation Row (RS): Attach A with sl st in first sc and sl st in each rem st across. Fasten off.

fringe
Tie in groups of 2 and 3 across each short side. Trim evenly.

embellishments
1. Following chart, left-handed crocheter starts at red dot and works from the inside out; right-handed crocheter starts at green dot and works from the outside in.

2. Place a sc in designated ch-1 sp and ch 3 between each sc. A black square denotes a sc in a ch-1 sp. When you get to the end of a row, turn work toward hand holding the hook.

3. **Progression for LH:** Starting at red dot, 2 sc. Turn; 2 sc. Turn; 3 sc. Turn; 4 sc. Turn; 5 sc. Turn; 6 sc. Turn; 7 sc. Turn; 6 sc. Fasten off — 35 sc.

4. **Progression for RH:** Starting at green dot, 7 sc. Turn; 7 sc. Turn; 6 sc. Turn; 5 sc. Turn; 4 sc. Turn; 3 sc. Turn; 2 sc. Turn; 1 sc. Fasten off — 35 sc.

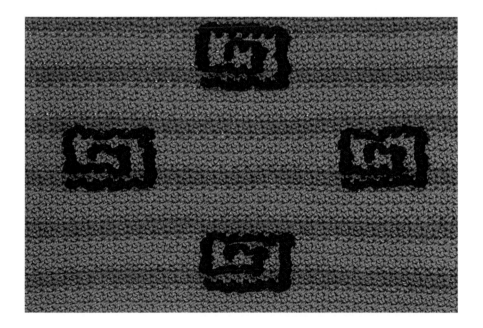

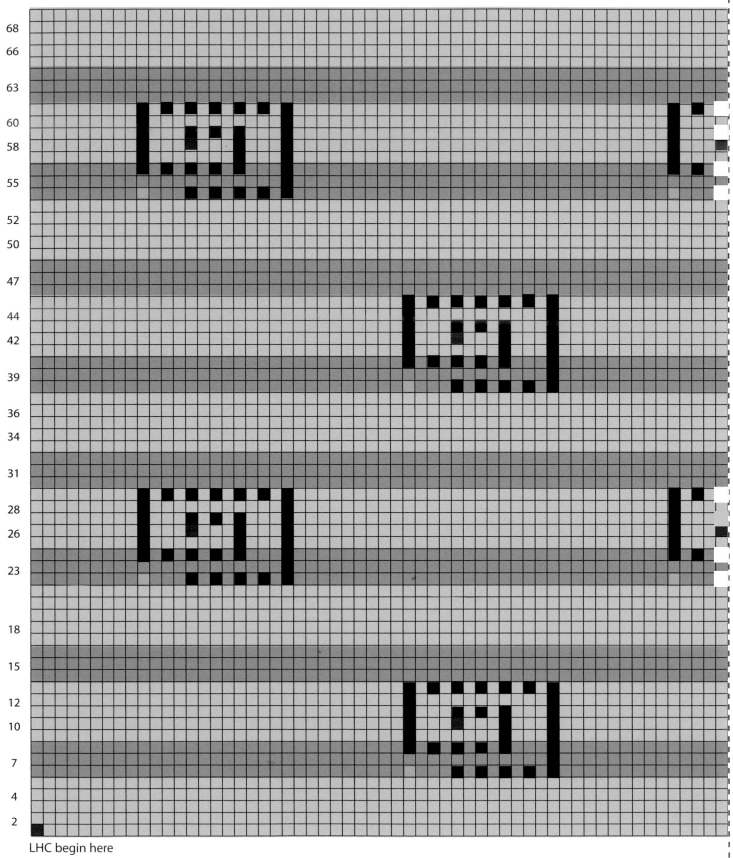

LHC begin here

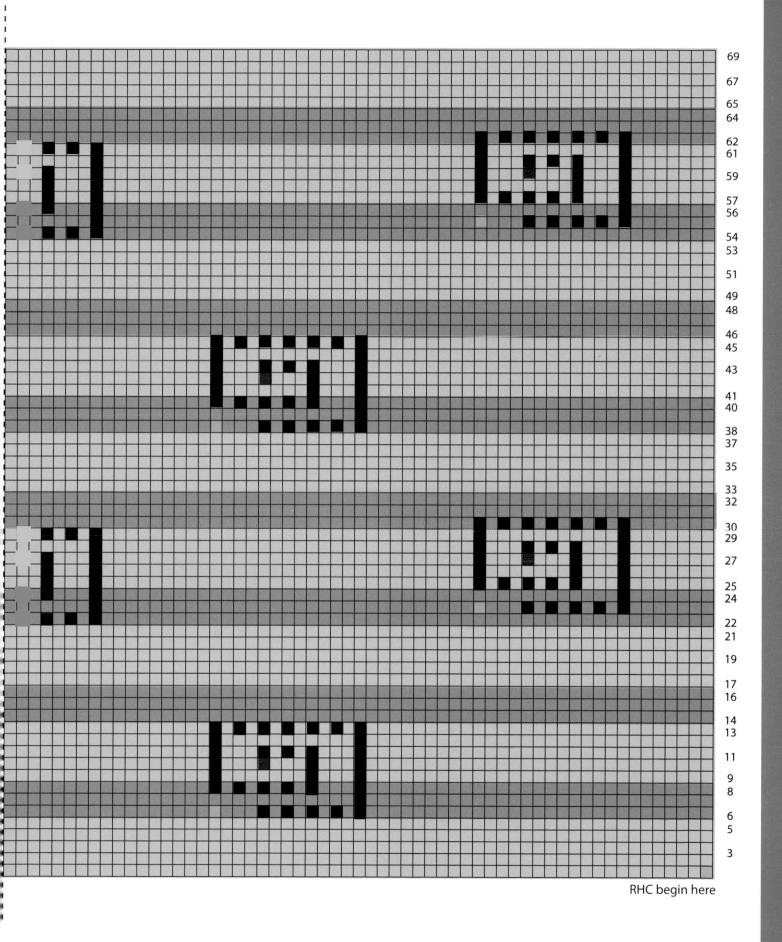

RHC begin here

square baskets

Again, you don't need a lot of numbers to take advantage of the Fibonacci system. These baskets incorporate just the first four numbers, 1-1-2-3, with a little artistic license. The sequence is actually 1-1-1-2-3, so I could add a second color and a little pizzazz.

skill level
■ ■ □ □
Easy

sizes
3½ (5½, 7½)" square x 5" tall

materials

 Worsted Weight Jute Twine (3.6 oz/75 yards per ball) Natural – 5 balls

 Cotton Crochet Thread Small amounts of: Red (A), Teal (B), Pink (C), Black (D)
• Crochet hooks, sizes C/2 (2.75 mm), H/8 (5 mm) and I/9 (5.5 mm) or size needed to obtain gauge
• Markers
• Tapestry needle to work in ends

gauge
5 rnds = approx 3½"

notes
1. Join each round with sl st in first sc, ch 1 and sc in same sl st as the join to begin each round.
2. While forming the bottom, keep a marker in the first st of each round and in each corner stitch. It makes keeping track of your stitches much easier.
3. When working with jute, hold the hook like a knife (under the palm) to lessen the tension on your hand.

instructions for all sizes
Foundation Rnd (all sizes): With medium hook ch 4, join with sl st to form ring.
Rnd 1: 8 sc in ring, join.
Rnd 2: Ch 1, sc in first sc, 3 sc in next sc, corner made, (sc in next sc, 3 sc in next sc) three times, all corners made, join — 16 sc.
Rnd 3: Ch 1, sc in each sc around, working 3 sc in center of each 3-sc corner group, join — 24 sc.
Rnds 4–5 (4–8, 4–11): Rep rnd 3. On last rnd, join through back lp — 40 (64, 88) sc.

Small basket (3½")

Medium basket (5½")

Note: For rounds 1, 4, 7, 9, 10, and 11 work in the back lps only.

Rnd 1: Working in back lps, ch 1, sc in each sc around, join through both lps.

Rnds 2: Working in both lps, ch 1, sc in each sc around, join through both lps.

Rnd 3: Working in both lps, ch 1, sc in each sc around, join through back lp.

Rnd 4: Working in back lps, ch 1, sc in each sc around, join through both lps.

Rnd 5: Working in both lps, ch 1, sc in each sc around, join through both lps.

Rnd 6: Working in both lps, ch 1, sc in each sc around, join through back lp.

Rnd 7: Working in back lps, ch 1, sc in each sc around, join through both lps.

Rnd 8: Working in both lps, ch 1, sc in each sc around, join through back lps.

Rnds 9–10: Working in back lps, ch 1, sc in each sc around, join through back lps.

Rnd 11: Working in back lps, ch 1, sc in each sc around, join through both lps.

Rnds 12–14: Working in both lps, ch 1, sc in each sc around, join through both lps.

Rnd 15: With largest hook, ch 1, sl st in both lps of each sc around, DO NOT JOIN. Cut yarn leaving a 6" tail and pull through lp with hook. Thread tail onto tapestry needle, insert needle from front to back under both lps of first st of round, pull through to back side, weave end through sts on back side. Fasten off.

trim

Color Sequences:

Small Basket: red, black, red, red, red.

Medium Basket: teal, black, teal, teal, teal.

Large Basket: pink, black, pink, pink, pink.

With smallest hook, beg at back where basket rnds were joined, starting on rnd 11 with hook pointing down, (sc, ch 1) in each sc around, end with sc in same st as first st of trim rnd, join. Fasten off. Rep on rnds 10, 9, 7, and 4. **Note:** Rnd 1 is not part of the Fibonacci sequence. It is worked in the back lp to help shape the basket.

Large basket (7½")

afghan
& pillows

3-5-8 was the Fibonacci sequence originally chosen for this project. But I wanted to have 45 rows. I also wanted to start and end each square with the same color, which required an uneven number of rows. So I fudged a bit, took creative license, and changed the sequence to 3-5-9 for the afghan and one side of the pillows.

On the other side of the pillows, the palindrome pattern is governed by stitches, not rows or inches. It goes like this: 21-34-55-89-144-89-55-34-21 alternating colors A and B from start to finish.

Palindrome pillow back

skill level

Beginner

sizes

Squares are 11¼" before borders
and joining
Afghan approx 51" x 51"
Pillows 12" square after stretching
over pillow forms

materials

Worsted Weight Yarn
(3.5 ounces/210 yards,
100 grams/192 meters
per skein):

Dark Purple (A) – 9 skeins
Light Purple (B) – 10 skeins
• Crochet hooks, sizes H/8
(5 mm) and I/9 (5.5 mm) or size
needed to obtain gauge
• Cardboard, 12" x 3"
• Three 12" pillow forms
• Stitch markers
• Tapestry needle to work in ends

gauge

16 sts = 4" and 16 rows = 5"

notes

1. To make squares with matching
gauges: Cut a piece of cardboard
12" x 3", mark off 11¼", and lay it
in your lap as you work. As often
as necessary, measure at the end
of a row for instant feedback.
Gently lay one side along the
11¼" line on the short side of the
cardboard. Without stretching, lay
the top end along the top edge of
the cardboard. Now feel with your
fingers how much hangs over the
other short edge (if any). It should
feel about the same each time. If
working too tight, loosen up a bit;
if working too loose, tighten up a
bit.
2. To change colors see notes on
page 104.

special stitch

Forked Cluster (FC):
First FC st of row: Ch 3 (counts
as dc), yo, insert hook into first
st, yo and pull through, yo, insert
hook into next st, yo and pull
through (5 lps on hook), [yo and
pull through 3 lps] twice.
FC subsequent sts: Yo, insert
hook into same st as previous FC,
yo and pull through, yo, insert
hook into next st, yo and pull
through, [yo and pull through 3
lps] twice.
FC corner: FC through last sc before corner sc, ch 1, FC in same sc
and corner sc, ch 1, FC in corner
sc, ch 1, FC in corner sc and next
sc, ch 1, proceed in pattern st to
end, sl st to top of beg ch-3.

instructions

Afghan and Pillow Squares
Note: Make 19 squares: five
5-stripes, five 9-stripes, five 15-
stripes, 2 solid dark purple, 2 solid
light purple — yields 16 squares
for the afghan and 3 for the pillows.
5-stripe color sequence #1: 9
rows A, 9 B, 9 A, 9 B, 9 A
9-stripe color sequence #2: 5 A, 5
B, 5 A, 5 B, 5 A, 5 B, 5 A, 5 B, 5 A
15-stripe color sequence #3: 3 A,

3 B, 3 A, 3 B, 3 A, 3 B, 3 A, 3 B, 3 A, 3 B, 3 A, 3 B, 3 A, 3 B, 3 A (Option: If desired, replace the solid squares with these 3-stripe color sequences: 15 A, 15 B, 15A, and 15 B, 15 A, 15 B.)

Foundation Row: Ch 37.
Row 1: With A and larger hook, sc in second ch from hook and each ch across. Turn — 36 sc.
Rows 2–45: Following color sequences, ch 1, sc in each sc across. Fasten off.

Edging for Squares

(RS) Using B and smaller hook, join with a sc and sc evenly around each square, placing 3 sc in each corner — 36 sc between corner scs. Hint: On row ends, place markers at regular intervals to help you space the sts evenly.

Joining Squares

Using following method and referring to photo for placement, join squares in 4 strips of 4, then join strips. Working with B on WS, join with sl st through both front lp of nearest square and back lp of farthest square, sl st in each pair of sc across. Fasten off.

Edging for Afghan

Rnd 1 (RS): With B and smaller hook, join with a sc and sc in each sc around, placing 3 sc in each corner st, sl st to beg sc. Fasten off, do not turn.
Rnd 2: With A, join with sl st to

any sc, ch 3 and work 1 rnd of FC sts, sl st to beg ch-3, do not turn.
Rnd 3: Ch 1 (counts as first sl st), sl st in each st around, sl st to beg sl st. Fasten off.

Palindrome Pillow Backs (Make 3)

The Fibonacci stitch sequence used is: (21 A, 34 B, 55 A, 89 B, 144 A, 89 B, 55 A, 34 B) three times, ending with 21 A, 36 B. It's interesting to note that the unplanned color pattern seems to break most often in the middle of the pillow.

Foundation Row: With A, ch 37.
Row 1: Sc in second ch from hook and next 20 ch (21 sts total), drop A, pick up B, sc in next 15 ch. Turn — 36 sc.
Row 2: Ch 1, sc in first 19 sc (34 sts total), drop B; pick up A, sc in last 17 sc. Turn.

Rows 3–45: Ch 1 and, following st counts, continue in Fibonacci sequence to end of pillow. Fasten off.

Edging

(RS) With B and smaller hook, join with a sc and sc evenly around, placing 3 sc in each corner st — 36 sc between corner scs.

Joining Pillow Front to Pillow Back

Rnd 1: With B and smaller hook, going through front lp of nearest side and back lp of farthest side at the same time, join with a sl st, ch 3 and work 1 rnd of FC around 3 sides. Insert pillow form and cont in pattern st on fourth side to end, sl st to beg ch-3, do not turn.
Rnd 2: Ch 1 (counts as first sl st), sl st in each st around, sl st to beg sl st. Fasten off.
Rep for other 2 pillows.

circles poncho

The Fibonacci sequence can be used with any shape, as this project made with circles illustrates. It utilizes three sequences (2-3-5-8, 8-5-3-2, and 8-5-3-5-8) plus five one-color circles to make up the body of the poncho. You could even throw in some smaller circles for good measure.

skill level

■■□□
Easy

size

One size fits most

materials

 Sport Weight Yarn (1.75 ounces/154 yards, 50 grams/140 meters per skein):

Light purple (A) – 3 skeins
Red (B) – 3 skeins
Yellow (C) – 3 skeins
Dark purple (D) – 3 skeins
Green (E) – 3 skeins
• Crochet hooks, sizes G/6 (4 mm) and K/10.5 (6.5 mm) or size needed to obtain gauge
• Safety pins
• Small amount contrasting yarn
• Tapestry needle to work in ends

gauge

18-round circle = 10" across

notes

1. To enlarge pattern, increase the number of circles.
2. End each round with sl st in first sc, and begin each round with ch 1 and sc in same sc as join.
3. A large hook is used with light - weight yarn to keep the fabric soft and drapy. Work loosely!
4. To change colors, see notes on page 104.

special stitch

Single Crochet 2 Stitches Together (Sc2tog): (Insert hook into next st, yo and pull through) twice, yo and pull through all 3 lps on hook.

circles

There are four designs in this poncho. One is 18 rounds in a single color, and three follow these Fibonacci sequences for number of rounds to crochet in each color: 2-3-5-8, 8-5-3-2 and 5-3-2-3-5.

Here are the color sequences:

5 circles
1 each of A, B, C, D, and E

5 circles 2-3-5-8
2A-3B-5C-8D
2B-3C-5D-8E
2C-3D-5E-8A
2D-3E-5A-8B
2E-3A-5B-8C

5 circles 8-5-3-2
8A-5B-3C-2D
8B-5C-3D-2E
8C-5D-3E-2A
8D-5E-3A-2B
8E-5A-3B-2C

5 circles 5-3-2-3
5A-3B-2C-3D-5E
5B-3C-2D-3E-5A
5C-3D-2E-3A-5B
5D-3E-2A-3B-5C
5E-3A-2B-3C-5D

instructions

Foundation Rnd: With larger hook, ch 4, join with sl st.

Rnd 1: Ch 1, 6 sc in ring, join — 6 sc.

Rnd 2: Ch 1, 2 sc in each sc, join — 12 sc.

Rnd 3: Ch 1, sc in same sc as join, 2 sc in next sc, *sc in next sc, 2 sc in next sc, rep from * around, join — 18 sc.

Rnd 4: Ch 1, sc in same sc as join and next sc, 2 sc in next sc, *sc in each of next 2 sc, 2 sc in next sc, rep from * around, join — 24 sc.

Rnd 5: Ch 1, sc in same sc as join and next 2 sc, 2 sc in next sc, *sc in each of next 3 sc, 2 sc in next sc, rep from * around, join — 30 sc.

Rnd 6: Ch 1, sc in same as join and in the next sc, 2 sc in the next sc, (4 sc, 2 sc in the next sc) 5 times, ending with 2 sc, join — 36 sts.

Rnd 7: Ch 1, sc in same as join, 2 sc in next sc, 4 sc, 2 sc in next sc, (5 sc, 2 sc in the next sc) 4 times, ending with 5 sc, join — 42 sts.

Rnd 8: Ch 1, sc in same as join, 3 sc, 2 sc in next sc, 5 sc, 2 sc in next sc, (6 sc, 2 sc in next sc) 4 times, ending with 3 sc, join — 48 sts.

Rnd 9: Ch 1, 2 sc in same sc as join, (7 sc, 2 sc in next sc) 2 times, 6 sc, 2 sc in next sc, (7 sc, 2 sc in next sc) 2 times, ending with 8 sc, join — 54 sts.

Rnd 10: Ch 1, sc in same sc as join, 3 sc, 2 sc in next sc, 11 sc, 2 sc in next sc, 5 sc, 2 sc in next sc, (7 sc, 2 sc in next sc) 2 times, 8 sc, 2 sc in next sc, ending with 6 sc, join — 60 sts.

Rnd 11: Ch 1, sc in same sc as join, 7 sc, 2 sc in next sc, 12 sc, 2 sc in next sc, 6 sc, 2 sc in next sc, (8 sc, 2 sc in next sc) 2 times, 9 sc, 2 sc in next sc, ending with 3 sc, join — 66 sts.

Rnd 12: Ch 1, sc in same as join, sc, 2 sc in next sc, (12 sc, 2 sc in next sc) 2 times, 5 sc, 2 sc in next sc, (9 sc, 2 sc in next sc) 2 times, ending with 11 sc, join — 72 sts.

Rnd 13: Ch 1, sc in same sc as join, 5 sc, 2 sc in next sc, 14 sc, 2 sc in next sc, 12 sc, 2 sc in next sc, 6 sc, 2 sc in next sc, 11 sc, 2 sc in next sc, 10 sc, 2 sc in next sc, ending with 7 sc, join — 78 sts.

Rnd 14: Ch 1, 2 sc in same as join, 12 sc, 2 sc in next sc, 13 sc, 2 sc in next sc, 15 sc, 2 sc in next sc, 6 sc, 2 sc in next sc, 12 sc, 2 sc in next sc, ending with 14 sc, join — 84 sts.

Rnd 15: Ch 1, sc in same as join, 3 sc, 2 sc in next sc, (15 sc, 2 sc in next sc) 2 times, 13 sc, 2 sc in next sc, 9 sc, 2 sc in next sc, 17 sc, 2 sc in next sc, ending with 5 sc — 90 sts.

Rnd 16: Ch 1, sc in same as join, 8 sc, 2 sc in next sc, 17 sc, 2 sc in next sc, 16 sc, 2 sc in next sc, 15 sc, 2 sc in next sc, 11 sc, 2 sc in next sc, 7 sc, 2 sc in next sc, ending with 9 sc — 96 sts.

Rnd 17: Ch 1, sc in same as join, 2 sc, 2 sc in next sc, 12 sc, 2 sc in next sc, 20 sc, 2 sc in next sc, 16 sc, 2 sc in next sc, 15 sc, 2 sc in next sc, 10 sc, 2 sc in next sc, ending with 14 sc — 102 sts.

Rnd 18: Ch 1, sc in same as join, 7 sc, 2 sc in next sc, 18 sc, 2 sc in next sc, 20 sc, 2 sc in next sc, (15 sc, 2 sc in next sc) 2 times, 13 sc, 2 sc in next sc, ending with 7 sc — 108 sts.

Rnd 19: Ch 1 (counts as sl st), sl st in next sc and each sc around, join to first ch-1. Fasten off.

to assemble

The model was made with one round of 6 overlapping circles, followed by one round of 9 circles, followed by random placement of the 5 rem circles. Leave about a 5" opening for the neck (the weight of the fabric will pull it open). On a large flat surface, lay out the circles until you think you are satisfied with the arrangement. When possible, hide joining seams under overlapping circles. Pin circles securely in place and try on the poncho, changing the arrangement if desired. With tapestry needle and contrasting yarn, baste around the edges of each overlapping circle. With tapestry needle and yarn to match, invisibly stitch circles tog where edges overlap, going through all layers.

neck edging

Rnd 1: With smaller hook and color of your choice, join with sc and sc in each sl st around neck opening, placing a 2sctog decrease at each intersection of circles. At the point where circles overlap, go through the last st of the top circle and the first st of the bottom circle at the same time. Sl st to beg sc.

Rnds 2–3: Ch 1, sc in each sc around, join.

Rnd 4: Ch 1 (counts as sl st), sl st in next sc and each sc around, join to beg sl st. Fasten off.

checkered rug

The checkerboard rug utilizes two simple asymmetrical sequences, 4-4-8-12-20-32, and 4-4-8-12-20-32-52, going in two directions at once. It's actually possible to go in many directions all at the same time. See the Challenges section at the end of this chapter.

skill level

Intermediate

size

Approx 30" x 41" (excluding fringe)

materials

Worsted Weight Yarn (4 ounces/190 yards, 113 grams/174 meters per skein):

Blue (A) – 3 skeins

Rose (B) – 4 skeins

• Crochet hooks, sizes I/9 (5.5 mm) and J/10 (6 mm) or size needed to obtain gauge

• Tapestry needle to work in ends

gauge

10 sts and 8 rows = 3"

notes

1. Leave a 6" tail at beginning and end of each row to be used as fringe.

2. Work first row of sc in foundation chain and rows 2-81 in back loop of each sc. Keep RS facing at all times, do not turn.

3. Work over strand not in use.

4. To change colors see notes on page 104. At each color change, check the back of the work for any slack and to make sure you haven't dropped/missed catching the unused strand. Give a gentle tug, being careful not to pull too tightly and pull rug out of shape.

5. **Special way to hold both yarns at once (see photos on page 95):** To better control the yarn, feed both the working strand and the carry-along yarn through your fingers as you work. It keeps the tension even and less of the carry along yarn is visible on the RS. **For RH and LH:** The working thread goes over your index finger, the carry-along yarn over the middle finger of your yarn-holding hand.

instructions for LHC

Foundation Row (RS): With larger hook and A, ch 132. Fasten off.

Rows 1–80: Follow chart on page 96-97 for colors and numbers of stitches. Here's a "cheat sheet" to make it easier to keep track of what you're doing.

Rows 1–4: 4A, 4B, 8A, 12B, 20A, 32B, 52A

Rows 5–8: 4B, 4A, 8B, 12A, 20B, 32A, 52B

Rows 9–16: 4A, 4B, 8A, 12B, 20A, 32B, 52A

Rows 17–28: 4B, 4A, 8B, 12A, 20B, 32A, 52B

Rows 29–48: 4A, 4B, 8A, 12B, 20A, 32B, 52A

Rows 49–80: 4B, 4A, 8B, 12A, 20B, 32A, 52B

Row 81: With smaller hook and A, sl st loosely in back lp of each sc across. Fasten off.

fringe

Tie in groups of four across. Trim evenly.

instructions for RHC
RHC

Rows 1-4: 52A, 32B, 20A, 12B, 8A, 4B, 4A

Rows 5-8: 52B, 32A, 20B, 12A, 8B, 4A, 4B

Rows 9-16: 52A, 32B, 20A, 12B, 8A, 4B, 4A

Rows 17-28: 52B, 32A, 20B, 12A, 8B, 4A, 4B

Rows 29-48: 52A, 32B, 20A, 12B, 8A, 4B, 4A

Rows 49-80: 52B, 32A, 20B, 12A, 8B, 4A, 4B

Row 81: With smaller hook and A, sl st loosely in back lp of each sc across. Fasten off.

fringe

Tie in groups of four across. Trim evenly.

working with two yarns at once

LHC

RHC

Checkerboard Pattern

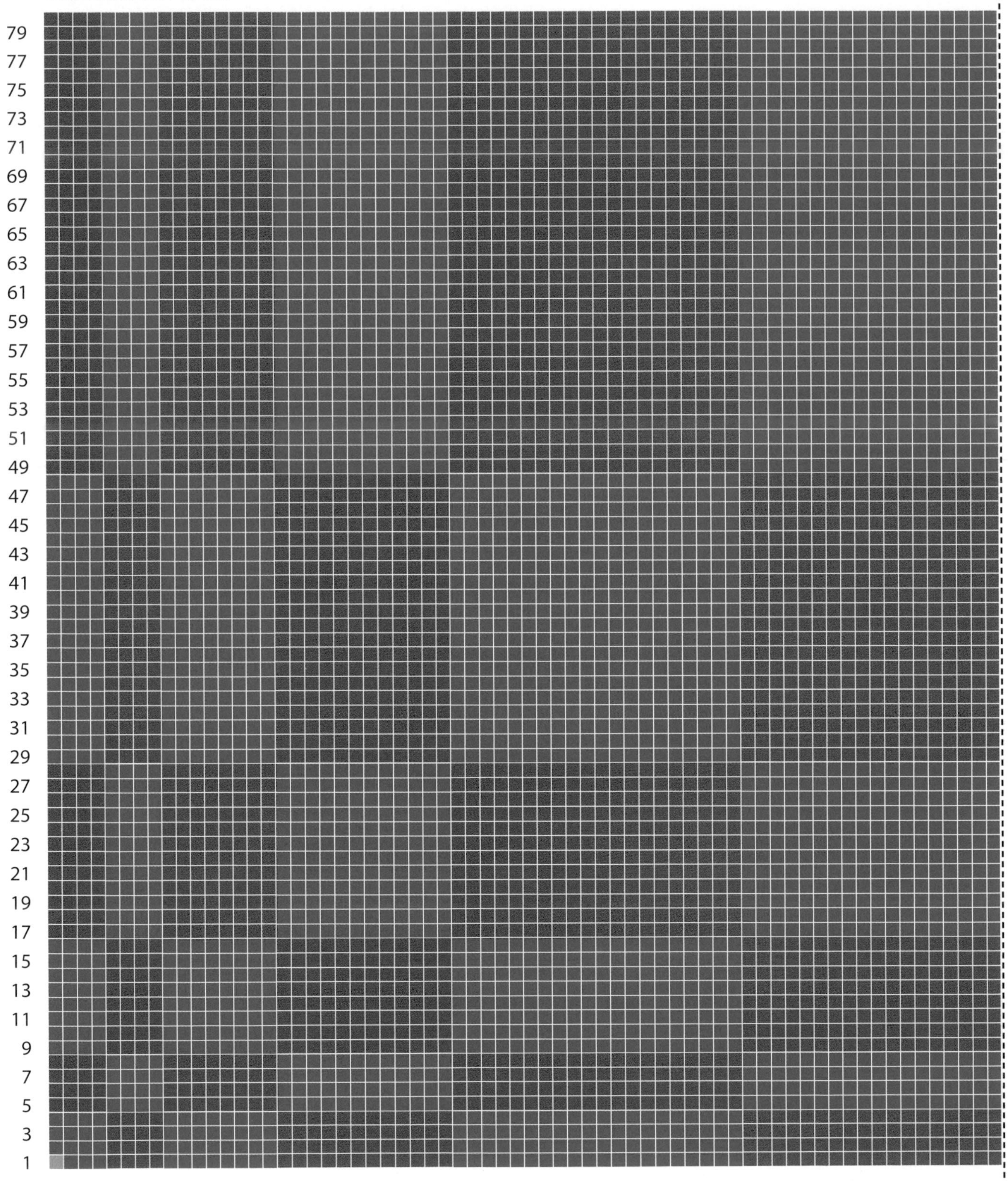

79
77
75
73
71
69
67
65
63
61
59
57
55
53
51
49
47
45
43
41
39
37
35
33
31
29
27
25
23
21
19
17
15
13
11
9
7
5
3
1

LHC begin here

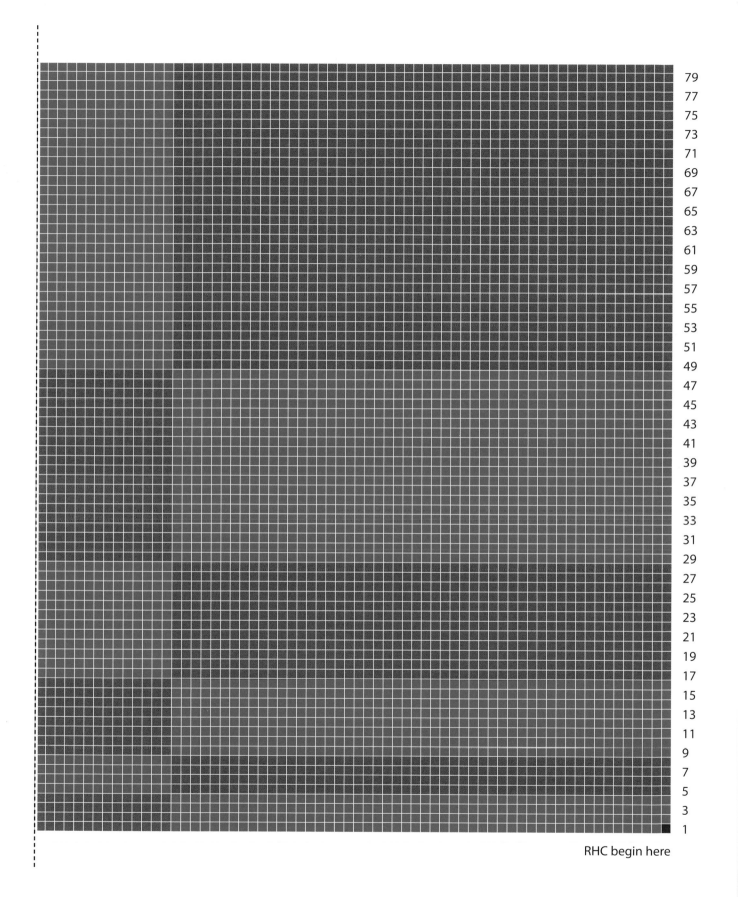

79
77
75
73
71
69
67
65
63
61
59
57
55
53
51
49
47
45
43
41
39
37
35
33
31
29
27
25
23
21
19
17
15
13
11
9
7
5
3
1

RHC begin here

fibonacci sequence challenges

1. Will some mathematical genius please come up with a formula to replace the cumbersome method used in rounds 6 to 18 of the circles poncho?

2. Inch-count wall hanging or rug: Using 5 colors, combine a Fibonacci sequence (or one of your own) with a golden rectangle. Each stripe is to be 1" wide.

3. Come up with a different arrangement for the afghan squares on page 86.

4. Stitch-count placemats: With as many as 7 colors, create colorful placemats using the palindrome stitch-count method described on page 84.

5. Make a poncho similar to the circles poncho, only use squares or rectangles or triangles (or a combination!), and incorporate a variety of yarns.

6. Tall and round or triangular baskets would be handsome and allow for more Fibonacci stripes than the square baskets. For a firm basket, use as small a hook as you can manage with the yarn of your choice.

7. With your own set of numbers, work out a design using the multiple sequences in Fig. 1.

8. Work out a design based on the artwork in Fig. 2.

advanced fibonacci designs

Fig. 1

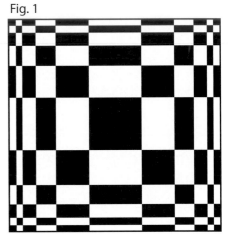

Fig. 2

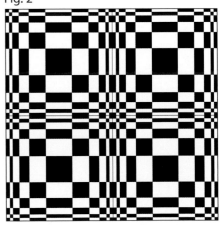

creating your own fibonacci designs

When making a standard checker-board you would mark equal inter-vals along each side of a square. For Fibonacci checkerboard art, mark your intervals along the sides using consecutive Fibonacci numbers. Start by marking two intervals of a one-unit length. Your next interval will be twice as long, followed by additional lengths that are three, five, and eight times as long.

Design Exercise: Use one color with a white background or two colors to create your own Fibonacci checkerboard design in the grid above (Fig. 1). Refer to Fig. 2 for an example of a colored design. Fig. 3 shows four of the colored squares combined to make a larger design.

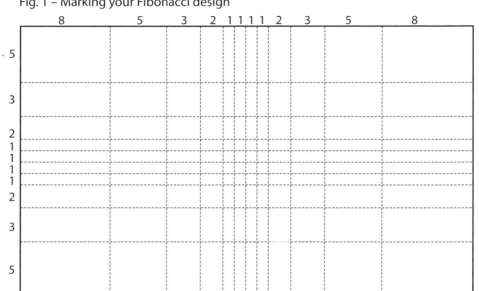

Fig. 1 – Marking your Fibonacci design

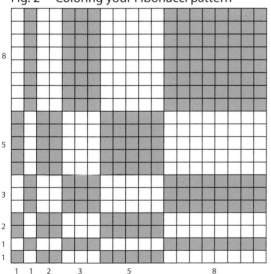

Fig. 2 – Coloring your Fibonacci pattern

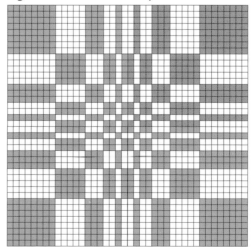

Fig. 3 – Combination of 4 patterns

stitch diagrams

making a chain

A chain starts with a slip knot (which does not count as a stitch). To make a chain, yarn over and pull through loop on hook.

working in the chain

Method A: Insert hook under back loop of chain.
Method B: Insert hook under top two loops of chain.

slip stitch

Insert hook, yarn over and pull loop through stitch and loop on hook.

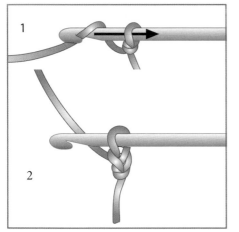

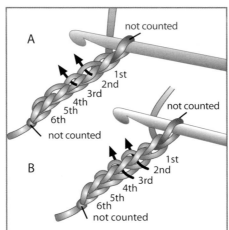

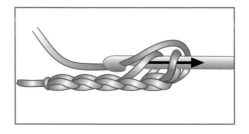

single crochet

Insert hook, yarn over and pull loop through, yarn over and pull through two loops on hook.

double crochet

Yarn over, insert hook, yarn over and pull loop through, yarn over and pull through two loops, yarn over and pull through rem two loops.

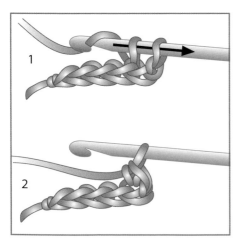

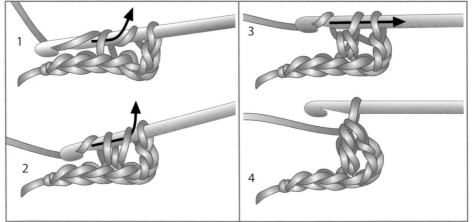

half double crochet

Yarn over and insert hook, yarn over and pull through loop. You will have three loops on hook. Yarn over and pull through all three loops on hook. You will have one loop remaining on hook ready to begin next stitch.

extended single crochet

Insert hook into next st, yo and pull through. Yo and pull through 2 Loops. Yo and pull through rem 2 Loops.

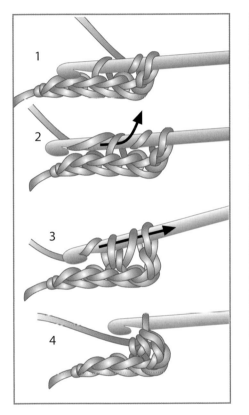

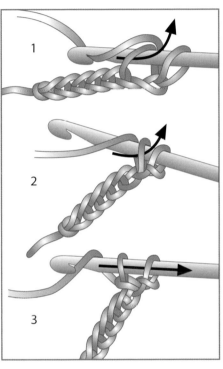

crossed double crochet

Skip one stitch, work one double crochet in next stitch. Work the second crochet back into the skipped stitch.

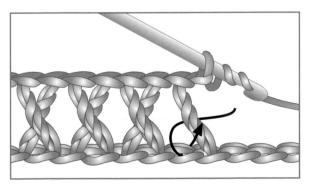

LH crossed double crochet

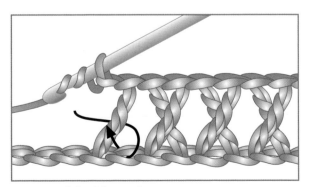

RH crossed double crochet

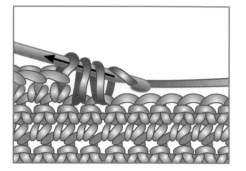

single crochet 2 stitches together (Sc2tog)

Insert hook in next stitch, yarn over and pull through loop. Insert hook into next stitch, yarn over and, pull through loop. You will have 3 loops on the hook. Yarn over and pull through all 3 loops on hook.

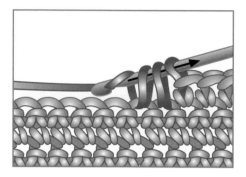

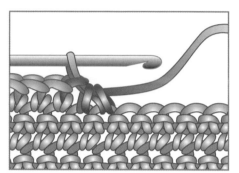

LH single crochet 2 together

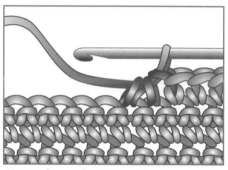

RH single crochet 2 together

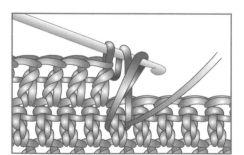

front post double crochet (FPdc)

Yarn over once. Insert the hook from the front, around the post, coming out again at the front. Yarn over and draw up one loop. Complete the double crochet as usual. This will create a raised stitch on the front of the fabric.

LH front post double crochet

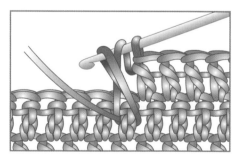

RH front post double crochet

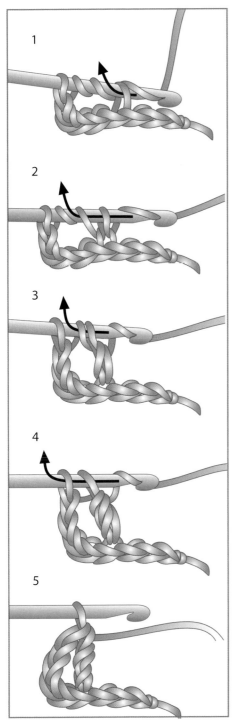

LH treble crochet

treble crochet

The turning chain is 4. Yarn over hook from back to front two times. Insert hook into both loops of next stitch or the back loop of next foundation chain, yarn over hook from back to front. Draw up yarn over through stitch. You will have four loops on hook. Yarn over hook from back to front and draw through first two loops on hook. Yarn over from back to front and draw it through two loops.

Yarn over from back to front and draw through last two loops. You will now have one loop remaining on hook ready to begin next stitch.

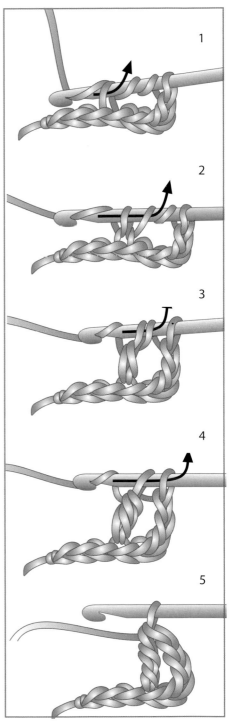

RH treble crochet

changing colors

Note: Always drop unused color to wrong side of work.

Sl st: Insert hook into next st (1 lp on hook), drop old color, pick up new color and pull through.

Sc: Insert hook into next st, yo and pull through (2 lps on hook), drop old color, pick up new color and pull through both lps.

Esc: Insert hook into next st, yo and pull through, (2 lps on hook), yo and pull through 1 lp (2 lps on hook), drop old color, pick up new color and pull through both lps.

Hdc: Yo, insert hook into next st, yo and pull through (3 lps on hook), drop old color, pick up new color and pull through all 3 lps.

Dc: Yo, insert hook into next st, yo and pull through (3 lps on hook), yo and pull through 2 lps (2 lps on hook), drop old color, pick up new color and pull through both lps.

Tr: Yo twice, insert hook into next st, yo and pull through (4 lps on hook), [yo and pull through 2 lps] twice (2 lps on hook), drop old color, pick up new color and pull through both lps.

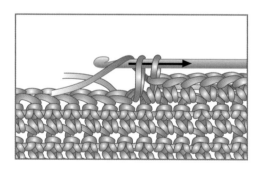

Changing colors

crochet abbreviations

[ ] – work instructions within brackets as many times as directed
( ) – work instructions within parentheses as many times as directed
* – rep the instructions following the single asterisk as directed
" – inches
approx – approximately
beg – begin(ning)
ch(s) – chain(s)
cont – continue
dc – double crochet
dtr – double triple crochet (yo 3 times)
Esc – extended single crochet
FC – forked cluster
FPdc – front post double crochet
hdc – half double crochet
L – left
LH – left-handed, left-hander
LHC – left-handed crocheter
lp(s) – loop(s)
mm – millimeter(s)
oz – ounce(s)
R – right
RH – right-handed, right-hander
RHC – right-handed crocheter
RS – right side
rem – remain(ing)
rep – repeat
rnd(s) – round(s)
sc – single crochet
Sc2tog – single crochet 2 stitches together
sk – skip
sl st – slip stitch
sp(s) – space(s)
st(s) – stitch(es)
tch – turning chain
tog – together
tr – triple crochet (yo 2 times)
ttr – triple triple crochet (yo 4 times)
Xdc – crossed double crochet
WS – wrong side
yo – yarn over (wrap yarn around hook)

useful information

crochet hook sizes

Millimeter Range	U.S. Size Range*
2.25 mm	B–1
2.75 mm	C–2
3.25 mm	D–3
3.5 mm	E–4
3.75 mm	F–5
4 mm	G–6
5 mm	H–8
5.5 mm	I–9
6 mm	J–10
6.5 mm	K–10½
8 mm	L–11
9 mm	N–13
10 mm	P–15
15 mm	Q

*Letter or number may vary. Rely on the millimeter (mm) size.

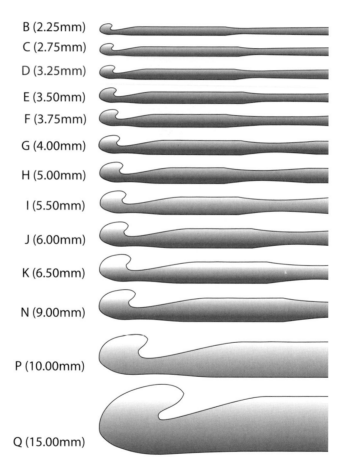

B (2.25mm)
C (2.75mm)
D (3.25mm)
E (3.50mm)
F (3.75mm)
G (4.00mm)
H (5.00mm)
I (5.50mm)
J (6.00mm)
K (6.50mm)
N (9.00mm)
P (10.00mm)
Q (15.00mm)

standard yarn weight system

Categories of yarn, gauge, and recommended needle and hook sizes

yarn weight symbol & category names	1 SUPER FINE	2 FINE	3 LIGHT	4 MEDIUM	5 BULKY	6 SUPER BULKY
type of yarns in catergory	sock, fingering, baby	sport, baby	DK, light worsted	worsted, afghan, aran	chunky, craft, rug	bulky, roving
crochet gauge* ranges in single crochet to 4 inch	21-32 sts	16-20 sts	12-17 sts	11-14 sts	8-11 sts	5-9 sts
recommended hook in metric size range	2.25-3.5 mm	3.5-4.5 mm	4.5-5.5 mm	5.5-6.5 mm	6.5-9 mm	9 mm and larger
recommended hook U.S. size range	B-1 to E-4	E-4 to G-7	G-7 to I-9	I-9 to K-10½	K-10½ to M-13	M-13 and larger

* Guidelines only: The above reflect the most commonly used gauges and needle or hook sizes for specific yarn categories.

yarn information

dragon curve projects

LUXURY SCARF (page 12)
Brown Sheep Nature Spun Sport Weight Yarn,
100% wool:
   #103 Deep Sea – 1.7 ounces/180 yards

DIAMOND SHAWL (page 14)
Brown Sheep Nature Spun Sport Weight Yarn,
100% wool:
   #730 Natural – 4 ounces/420 yards
   N27 Monument Green – 4 yards
   #207 Alpine Violet – 13 yards
   #205 Regal Purple – 23 yards

CRAFT TOTE FOR ALL REASONS (page 18)
Plymouth Encore Worsted Weight Yarn,
75% acrylic, 25% wool:
   #1383 Orange – 7 ounces/400 yards
   #1382 Lemon – 2.5 ounces/145 yards
   #1385 Magenta – 3.5 ounces/200 yards
   #3335 Lime – 2.5 ounces/145 yards

JUTE DOORMAT (page 22)
Lehigh #6105 Medium Weight Jute Twine:
   Natural – 25 ounces/1615 yards

RUFFLES AFGHAN (page 26)
Brown Sheep Nature Spun Sport Weight Yarn,
100% wool:
   N30 Nordic Blue – 16 ounces/1685 yards
   #202 Mango – 13 ounces/1370 yards

LABYRINTH (page 30)
Brown Sheep Lambs Pride Worsted Weight Yarn,
100% wool:
   M102 Orchid Thistle – 3 ounces/145 yards
Patons Cha Cha Super Bulky Weight Yarn,
100% nylon:
   #02011 Waltz – 3 ounces/135 yards

golden ratio projects

GOLDEN SCARF (page 40)
Plymouth Encore Worsted Weight Yarn,
75% acrylic, 25% wool:
   #9620 Blue – 1.75 ounces/100 yards
Plymouth Encore Colors Worsted Weight Yarn,
75% acrylic, 25% wool:
   #7091 Blue Variegated – 2 ounces/115 yards

SUMMER WALL HANGING (page 42)
Brown Sheep Lamb's Pride Worsted Weight Yarn,
85% mohair/15 % mohair:
   M22 Autumn Harvest – 3.5 ounces/170 yards
   M155 Lemon – 5 ounces/240 yards
Moda Dea Cache Bulky Weight Yarn, 75%
Wool/22% Acrylic/3% polyester:
   #2347 Wink – 17 yards

STAR AFGHAN (page 46)
Brown Sheep Lamb's Pride Worsted Weight Yarn,
85% wool/15% mohair:
   M102 Orchid Thistle – 26 ounces/1245 yards
   M28 Chianti – 17 ounces/815 yards

FLOWER POWER PILLOW (page 50)
Brown Sheep Lamb's Pride Worsted Weight Yarn,
85% wool/15% mohair:
    M62 Amethyst – 14 ounces/665 yards
    M22 Autumn Harvest – 4 ounces/190 yards
    M191 Kiwi – 6 ounces/285 yards

PUZZLE PLACEMATS (page 54)
Lily Sugar'n Cream Yarn, 100% cotton:
    #01742 Hot Blue – 9 ounces/435 yards
    #01712 Hot Green – 6 ounces/290 yards
    #01740 Hot Pink – 3 ounces/145 yards

GARDEN PONCHO (page 60)
Brown Sheep Nature Spun Worsted Weight Yarn,
100% wool:
    N25 Enchanted Forest – 6 ounces/425 yards
    N17 French Clay – 2 ounces/145 yards
    N27 Monument Green – 7 ounces/500 yards
    N56 Meadow Green – 3 ounces/215 yards

fibonacci projects
SCARLET SCARF (page 72)
Brown Sheep Wildfoote Sock Yarn, 75% washable
wool/25% nylon:
    SY26 Blue Blood Red – 1.2 ounces/145 yards
    SY300 Ragtime – 1.4 ounces/170 yards

STRIPED RUG (page 74)
Red Heart Classic Worsted Weight Yarn,
100% acrylic:
    #336 Warm Brown – 7 ounces/385 yards
    #401 Nickel – 4 ounces/220 yards

TLC Essentials Worsted Weight Yarn,
100% acrylic:
    #2913 Ranch Red – 1.5 ounces/80 yards

SQUARE BASKETS (page 80)
Lehigh #6105 Medium Weight Jute Twine:
    Natural – 15 ounces/312 yards
J & P Coats Royale Fashion Crochet Thread,
size 3, 100% Cotton 150 yards each:
    #6 Scarlett
    #65 Warm Teal
    #775 Warm Rose
    #12 Black

AFGHAN & PILLOW (page 84)
Plymouth Galway Highland Heather Worsted
Weight Yarn, 100% wool:
    #743 Dark Purple – 9 skeins/1890 yards
    #718 Light Purple – 10 skeins/2100 yards

CIRCLES PONCHO (page 88)
Brown Sheep Top of the Lamb Single Ply Sport
Weight Yarn, 100% wool:
    #465 Future Purple – 3.75 ounces/340 yards
    #420 Red Baron – 3.75 ounces/340 yards
    #414 Saffron – 3.75 ounces/340 yards
    #462 Great Grape – 4 ounces/360 yards
    #403 Appletree – 3.75 ounces/340 yards

CHECKERED RUG (page 92)
Brown Sheep Top of the Lamb Single Ply Sport
Weight Yarn, 100% wool,
    #310 Peacock – 12 ounces/575 yards
    #186 Dusty Rose – 13 ounces/620 yards

The projects in this book were made from various weights of yarn. Several different
brands of yarn in the weight specified for each project may be used. It is best to refer to the yardage /meters when determining how many balls or skeins to purchase.
Remember, to arrive at the finished size be sure to check your gauge.

index

resources

yarn & supplies

American Plastics
Round, hollow plastic tubing, ½" outside diameter, ¼" inside diameter
800-448-2234
www.americanplasticscorp.com

Bead Heaven
Wire-wrapped beads
Wholesale only, contact for a store near you.
212-376-1580
www.halcraft.com

Brown Sheep Yarn Company
Beautiful yarns
Wholesale only, contact for a store near you.
800-826-9136
www.brownsheep.com

Coats & Clark
Beautiful yarns
800-648-1479
www.coatsandclark.com

Lehigh
Jute twine
Wholesale only, contact for a store near you.
610-966-9702
www.lehighgroup.com

Moda Dea
Beautiful yarns
800-648-1479
www.modadea.com

Patons
Beautiful yarns
888-368-8401
www.patonsyarns.com

Plymouth Yarn Company
Beautiful yarns
Wholesale only, contact for a store near you.
800-523-8932
www.plymouthyarn.com

books

Dragon Curves, Labyrinths
Here Be Dragons Series
Steve Plummer, Ben Ashforth and Pat Ashforth. *Dragonometry, an introduction to Dragon Curves*
—*Scaled Down, instructions for making smaller items*
—*Scaled Up, instructions for an afghan or wall hanging*
Assign Publications, Colne, Lancashire England, 2002
01282 864273
www.woollythoughts.com

Virginia Westerbury. *Labyrinths: Ancient Paths of Wisdom and Peace.* Da Capo Press, Cambridge, MA, 2001.
617-252-5200
www.dacapopress.com

Golden Ratio and Fibonacci Sequence
Bezuszka, Stanley, Margaret Kenney and Linda Silvey. *Designs From Mathematical Patterns.* Dale Seymour Publications, div. of Pearson Learning, Parsippany, NJ, 1990.
www. amazon.com

Boles, Martha and Rochelle Newman *The Surface Plane: The Golden Relationship: Art, Math, and Nature.* Pythagorean Press, Bradford, MA, 1992.
800-321-3106
www.pearsonlearning.com

Garland, Trudi Hammel. *Fascinating Fibonaccis: Mystery and Magic in Numbers.* Dale Seymour Publications, div. of Pearson Learning, Parsippany, NJ, 1987.
800-321-3106.
http://k12catalog.pearson.com/co_home.cfm?site_id=11

Livio, Mario. *The Golden Ratio.* Broadway Books, div. of Random House, New York, NY, 2002.
800-733-3000
www.broadwaybooks.com

Newman, Rochelle and Martha Bowles. *Universal Patterns: The Golden Relationship: Art, Math and Nature,* Pythagorean Press, Bradford, MA, 1992.
978-372-3129
www.amazon.com

websites

Dragon Curves

http://en.wikipedia.org/wiki/Dragon_curve

www.seanet.com/~garyteachout/dragon.html

www.woollythoughts.com

Labyrinths

http://www.crystalinks.com/labyrinths.html

Fibonacci Sequence and Golden Ratio

http://en.wikipedia.org/wiki/Golden_ratio

http://en.wikipedia.org/wiki/Fibonacci

http://library.thinkquest.org/C005449/home.html

http://mathforum.org/drmath/faq/faq.goldenratio.html

http://mathforum.org/drmath/tocs/golden.high.html

www.mcs.surrey.ac.uk/Personal/R.Knott/Fibonacci

Yarn Standards

www.yarnstandards.com

notes